To Arlene

Dan B Derker

2024

My
GOD
is Only Good

An Easy-Read to Perception Change

Dr. C. Thomas Anderson

The Word for Winners©
P.O. Box 22229
Mesa, AZ 85277
thewordforwinners.com
(480) 669-0102

ISBN-10: 1645509028
ISBN-13: 9781645509028

My God *is Only Good*
An Easy-Read to Perception Change
Dr. C. Thomas Anderson

Becomingamillionairegodsway.com

Editor: Shelley Anne Johnson
Graphic Designer: Paul Howalt

Dr. C. thomas Anderson

becomingamillionairegodsway.com

Becomingamillionairegodsway.shop

 **becomingamillionairegodsway.TV**

 **Dr.C.ThomasAnderson**

Drcthomasanderson

DrCthomasA

My GOD is Only Good

Table of Contents

Introduction to
My God *is* *Only* *Good*

³Trust in the LORD with all your heart, and lean not on your own understanding... (Prov. 3:5 NKJ).

This was an audible word I received from God that set my mind and heart in motion on a journey to understand my God is only good. There is no darkness in Him at all. Through 46 years of studying the ancient Hebrew sages and rabbis' writings, I found the answers. God is good!

The belief that God kills, steals and destroys was created by religion to stop your ability to trust God with your whole heart. Seeing God as only good is the only way you can trust Him with your eternity.

Here's a thought: killing, stealing, destroying, conflict, intolerance, and darkness cannot, by definition, exist in the presence of true light and true spirituality. Therefore, my God has no darkness in Him.

⁵This is the message which we have heard from Him and <u>declare</u> to you, that God is light and in Him is no darkness <u>at all</u> (1 John 1:5).

"God is light and in Him is no darkness" is a complete sentence, but the writer felt it necessary to add *"<u>at all</u>"* to the end of the sentence.

God is the true Light and the true Spirit Who cannot, did not, could not, and will not ever be part of religion, division, disunity, killing, stealing or destroying.

Please allow me to say, that as I write this, I must explain that there is a difference between a religious institution and God's House, His Church. The Church is what Jesus died for. (*On this Rock, I will build My Church, Matt. 16:18.*) If the Church teaches the Word of God, if it teaches God's goodness, His love, His mercy and His works; if it teaches you to do good, with salvation through Christ, it is God's true House. Religious institutions are birthed out of controlling the flesh to keep religious law.

Religion fosters hate, war and genocide, all in the name of a god. (Not my God!) My God, the Author of divine wisdom, can only foster harmony, love and peace, making no distinction between personal beliefs, race, bank accounts, or education. If any religion displays any form of hostility or division of people, and if it does not generate light, love and life, there's something terribly wrong!

My God created heaven (invisible reality) and from it, earth, the visible reality. He did not create hell. (Man did.) My God did not create religion. Religion is a man-made invention which only brings separation, disunity and destruction of societies. Religion has spilled more blood than any disease or crimes combined.

My God has true light, love, and life in His mind and heart for man and offers to us unconditional love and kindness 24/7.

**Let's embark on a soul
and perception change,
without changing the words of God,
TOGETHER!**

God is Good and Only Good
Chapter 1

**God is light;
In Him there is no darkness at all.**
(1 John 1:5 NKJ)

This book should never have needed to be written, but religion, and the enemy have tainted our perception of our God right from Genesis 1:1.

[1]In the beginning God created the heavens and the earth. (Not Hell)

Through the whole creation process, all that God made was good. Ten times God created and said, "It is good." Ten is related to God's name, Yod, or expanded name, Yod Hei Vov Hei. Yod means the following and this is what we bring to the church, His House, the whole tenth or Yod:

All of which is produced by Christ in you and through you by salvation.

1) Tree of Life (Jesus)
2) The Anointed Christ (Jesus)
3) God's First-Fruit (Jesus)
4) God's Word Became Flesh (Jesus)
5) Our First-Fruit, His 10th, the tithe, Yod, Jesus brought to the House as His tithe, given in His House by us to build the Kingdom.

He put His tithe, His tenth, (our first-fruit) into our hands to test our hearts, and see if we would bring it to His House.

[10]Bring the whole tithe into the storehouse (Mal. 3:10).

We cannot give the tithe. We are only instructed to *bring* the 10th to His House. The tithe has always been God's but entrusted to us. How else could we rob God if it wasn't already His?

[8]"Will a man rob God? Yet you have robbed Me! But you say, 'In what way have we

robbed You?' In tithes and offerings" (Mal. 3:8).

All five meanings of Yod lead to good, love, light and life. Absolutely no darkness, death, destruction or negative is associated with any of the 22 Hebrew letters from which all our text comes. God created heaven and earth with no reference to the creation of hell, death, sickness, destruction or trouble. Hell, and all its attributes, was created by man's deception of believed lies of the enemy.

"Did God really say...?" (Gen 3:1 NIV)

To further explain, *In the beginning God created the heavens and earth (Gen. 1:1),* the visible and the invisible *...and darkness was... (Gen 1:2).* Period! Nothing else was created until God speaks light.

Darkness is the absence of the power and/or light of God. Our idea of hell is darkness. Satan and his fallen angels (demons) are committed to the emptiness of nothingness which is referred to in the Bible as Sheol and Hades, and translated as the <u>absence of light</u>.

Religion came up with the word *hell* for people who don't receive Christ or the light of God.

Life itself cannot be destroyed; only the flesh can. So a soul and spirit will live somewhere eternally, either in the presence of God with Christ or in eternal darkness with nothing. What that really means, we don't know. It is simply the absence of light.

One explanation, looking at the natural rather than the supernatural, is the mark of Cain in a natural setting. Cain left all of the light of God and simply lived in humanism. He became his own god or lived completely in dark without the light of God. We can say this about a great deal of the world today.

The reason people think of hell as fire and brimstone is because religion has taught them this. Jesus spoke of hell in Aramaic expressions. Jesus was amplifying that hell is not a place to go and live in eternal darkness.

God does motivate us to accept salvation in three ways: fear, reward and intrinsic. Through fear of eternal darkness, reward of promises, and intrinsic, "I just know that God is good," or "I just know God is the way."

That's the way I got saved! My motivation was that *I just knew* *God was the way,* probably based on my childhood. I was reared by my grandmother who was saved, not religious, but she loved God. She built and was committed to the little church in which I grew up.

Religion has used fire and brimstone to explain and utilize fear for salvation, but in reality, hell can't be fire or physical pain or physical torment because the soul and spirit could never experience these, only the flesh and the flesh is left here on the earth as dust. So the eternal soul that is not saved will live in the emptiness of nothingness. I can't think of anything worse! Prisons use isolation and darkness as the most severe punishment.

This book is part of a series to change your perceptions of the Bible without changing the words of God. Proverbs 3:5-6 says:

⁵Trust in the LORD with all your heart, and lean not on your own understanding; ⁶In all your ways acknowledge Him, and He shall direct your paths (NKJ).

**How can you trust God
with all your heart
if you believe God is good and evil?
God, Who has no darkness in Him!**

*God is light; In Him there is <u>no darkness
at all</u> (1 John 1:5 NKJ).*

Darkness cannot comprehend the light.

Seek understanding so you can do the wisdom of God in your life. Understanding the Word of God is critical to the "doing of His Word". *...be doers of the Word... (James 1:22 NKJ).*

**We only do what we understand,
not what we know.**

Proverbs 4:7 says,

[7]Wisdom is the principal thing; therefore get wisdom (NKJ).

Seek wisdom, and with it, gain under-standing.

9

[7]...and in all your getting, get under-standing (Prov. 4:7 NKJ).

A child must understand why <u>not</u> to chase a ball into the street, not just, "Don't do it."

It is Jesus (Who is the Word of God) Who said <u>God is good</u>. In essence, God said, "I Am good." God is I Am, or if you will, He *IS*, not was or will be, but *IS* always *IS*. Therefore God is never changing and *IS*, has been, and always will be good. Jesus said,

[49]"I don't speak on My own. I say only what the Father Who sent Me has told me to say" (John 12:49 CEV).

Jesus, the Word, is what God said! Jesus said it!

[18]"No one is good but One, that is God" (Mark 10:18 NKJ).

Jesus said, or the Word of God says,

[10]"The thief does not come except to steal, and to kill, and to destroy. I have come that

they may have life, and that they may have it more abundantly (John 10:10 NKJ).

Now two questions remain…

1) When did Jesus come?

And

2) When did the enemy come?

To find the answer to the first question, we need to go to Genesis.

⁹The Tree of <u>Life</u> was also in the midst of the Garden… (Gen. 2:9 NKJ).

Jesus <u>is</u> the Tree of <u>Life</u>.

So the answer to "When did Jesus come?" is Jesus was <u>in the Garden</u> as the Tree of Life! He is the Way, the Truth and the <u>Life</u>.

"⁶No one comes to the Father except by Me" (John 14:6 NKJ).

Okay, Jesus, the Tree of Life, came to the Garden. Why! To bring life and life more abundant so man could have chosen life (the Tree of Life) instead of eating from the Tree of Good and Evil. The Bible says in John 1:1,

¹In the beginning was the Word, and the Word was with God, and the Word was God. ² He was in the beginning with God. ³All things were made through Him, and without Him nothing was made that was made (John 1:1-3 NKJ).

There it is, *in the beginning*, just as in John 10:10, Jesus states,

"I am come that they may have life, and they may have it more abundantly."

So from the foundation of time, God's plan for man was life and life more abundant.

This was God's will, His plan, from the foundation of time for mankind. So when we read negatives in the Bible, like God did evil, it is not God, but it is the evil one.

10The thief does not come except to <u>steal</u>, and to <u>kill</u>, and to <u>destroy</u> (John 10:10 NKJ).

To answer the second question, "When did the enemy come?" Let's look at the fall of mankind. Lucifer, the greatest of the angels, was stationed <u>in the Garden</u> to do the bidding of God's Word.

**God would never put a viper
in man's back yard to kill him.**

Lucifer was placed there to aid and assist man. Angels do the bidding of God's Word.

20Praise the Lord, you His angels, you mighty ones <u>who do His bidding</u>, who obey His Word (Ps. 103:20 NIV).

But Lucifer, with free will, entered into pride and said,

^{14}*"I will ascend above the heights of the clouds, I will be like the Most High" (Is. 14:14 NKJ).*

By the act of his will, Lucifer chose darkness, and he became Satan in the Garden. He deceived man to give up his dominion and authority, thus, killing, stealing, and destroying entered the world of man. That dominion and authority was used by Satan to kill, steal and destroy and worked all the way from the Garden to the cross of Calvary.

God had to hold His own hands back (had to allow) until He could redeem mankind and every sin could be committed on the face of this earth. Then in the fullness of time, He sent Jesus to this earth, and at the cross of Calvary, Jesus took past, present and future sins away from all of us. He covered us all in His righteousness. He went into hell, took all of the darkness into hell, took back everything the enemy had ever stolen, and He gave it back to us. He gave dominion and authority back to God's kids once again.

Lucifer, in the Garden, was in envy, and envy is the root of all evil.

   [2] *"You must not eat of the fruit from the tree that is in the middle of the Garden... or you will die" (Gen. 3:3 NIV).*

   God did not say, *"If you eat..., I will kill you."* No, He was saying, *"If you eat..., you will produce death by the decision you make."* God did not create robots. He gave man a free will. He wanted a bride who would love Him, unconditionally.

   When we read about killing, stealing and destroying in the Bible, it was done by the enemy who comes to kill, steal and destroy (John 10:10). We have a wrong perception of God and the Bible, especially the Old Testament writings, and the inability to translate it accurately.

   Now let me take this deeper. Kenneth Hagin revealed that the ancient Hebrew, the origin of the Bible, along with the Aramaic, was translated into Greek and then English. His research revealed that the original Ancient

Hebrew has no permissive verbs, only causative verbs. So when we read that God caused death, God killed, or God destroyed, it should be translated,

God <u>had to permit</u> the negative to take place because God gave dominion and authority to Adam and Eve.

Adam and Eve were deceived and gave their God-given dominion and authority up to Satan. Now God was bound by His Word to allow or to permit that dominion and authority to remain in Satan's hands until Jesus was crucified. That's when Satan was defeated.

This is how dominion and authority were given to Adam and Eve but lost to the enemy in the Garden. Lucifer became Satan and had dominion and authority all the way to the death and burial of Jesus. Jesus then overcame, claimed back from hell all that was lost, and resurrected to total victory. With Satan defeated, God re-established dominion and authority to His kids. Satan was left without resources or authority and put under our feet.

Keep him under your feet
by never believing his lies.

And, yet religion still teaches that the enemy has power, but that's not true. He only has power if you or I lend it to him by believing his lies that create fear in us and empower him in our lives. <u>Your</u> greatest fear will come upon you.

25For the thing <u>I</u> <u>greatly</u> <u>feared</u> has come upon me. And what <u>I</u> dreaded has happened to me (Job 3:25 NKJ).

Now you can see that God is good, and always was good. Evil and hell are the devil's creation through our decisions and beliefs. God sent Jesus. God spoke Jesus, (His Word) in the beginning to bring life and life more abundant through the

1) <u>Tree of Life (Jesus)</u>
2) The <u>Anointed Christ (Jesus)</u>
3) <u>God's First-Fruit (Jesus)</u>
4) <u>God's Word Became Flesh (Jesus)</u>

5) Our First-Fruit, His 10th, the tithe, Yod, Jesus brought to the House as His tithe, given in His House by us to build the Kingdom of God.

All of Yod, or the tenth, are still producing a harvest for Him as each person gets saved yet today. These five meanings of Yod cannot be separated, but must all be applied to the meaning, of Yod, God's first name.

Looking a little deeper, allow me to bring some understanding to the mark of Cain. What was it? Cain killed his brother, Abel. This was Satan's second victory to stop any generational authority to continue. (The first was in the Garden when he deceived Eve into eating the apple.) Actually, Cain opened himself up to have a mark put on him, and then he blamed God. His decision, by the act of his free will, caused him to receive the mark of the world. God <u>had to allow</u> this by Cain's free will.

¹⁵Then the LORD put a mark on Cain so that no one who found him would kill him (Gen. 4:15 NIV).

The mark meant a total separation from the goodness of God. Remember this, God never <u>causes</u>, <u>but</u> <u>has</u> <u>to</u> <u>allow</u> because authority was taken from Adam and Eve, and now Satan could kill, steal, and destroy.

15...the LORD said to him, "Not so; anyone who kills Cain will suffer vengeance seven times over." Then the LORD put a mark on Cain so that no one who found him would kill him (Gen. 4:15 NIV).

Why?

**Because God will always
be the Author of life.**

Cain (man) then entered natural love (multiple wives), natural joy, and natural music that ministers to the natural soul of man. He sought natural love, and natural peace and lost all of God's promises. Thus, all of God's promises were no longer available to him because he was looking to the natural.

Cain (man) entered into natural wealth to live in corrupt cities and live off the backs of the rural righteous (right-living) sowers and reapers! It's still going on today. The cities exist because of a few righteous churches and believers in them. Corruption thrives and even corruption votes in many corrupt leaders. Thank God for the Founding Fathers and the Electoral College to give the rural a voice of rightness and to balance out the corrupt cities' leading. Cain was the builder of cities. Thomas Jefferson said it this way,

"When we get piled upon one another in large cities, as in Europe, we shall become as corrupt as Europe."

Cain was of the natural inventors (to ease the labors), natural health (man's medical healing), and natural favor (favor by manipulation, conning and lies). Not that all of these are bad, but they left the power of God's health, wealth, joy, peace, and favor, the values of morality, and the values of the divine nature of God and His goodness. Yet to stay balanced, not everyone in cities, not all music, not all inventions, not all relationships are corrupt.

Remember, they ate of the Tree of Good *and* Evil, so some GOOD and some evil.

God's love can't fail, but natural love is conditional. I love you, if... or because... God's love is, "I love you because you exist." Remember Genesis 1:2,

²...and darkness was...

Darkness was not created. First John 1:5 says,

⁵...in Him is no darkness at all.

Light is. Darkness isn't, until we create it. Remember hell was not created until man created his own fate and ate of the Tree of Good and Evil.

I said all this not to change the Word of God, but to change your perception of the Word of God. When you read through the Old Testament, and you read God did negative things to mankind, realize, it's in the translation of Hebrew and Aramaic. There are no permissive verbs in the Hebrew, only causative. So when you read that God killed or destroyed, it should read that God <u>had to allow</u> because He was bound to His Word. Dominion and authority on earth was now in the hands of the enemy to kill, steal, and destroy. (John 10:10) This finally allows us to believe that God has been, is, and will always be good.

**The Old Testament appears
to blame God for evil,
and the Church has bought into it.
Thus a false gospel.**

God has never killed anyone.

God has never sent anyone to hell.

Any Questions?
Chapter 2

Here are a few questions for you:

Did God send Jesus to earth to correct <u>God's</u> mistakes?

Or

Was He sent to die for <u>our</u> mistakes?

Ponder the questions below. Where do you stand? What do you believe?

Question #1

Did God murder millions of people in the flood, and break His own commandment of *Thou shalt not kill?* And if God caused the storms, then when Jesus rebuked the winds and waves or storm, was Jesus rebuking God?

Answer to Question #1

Here are things to consider. In short,

Who is the author of life?
Who is the author of death?

And the LᵏRD *God formed man of the dust of the ground, and breathed into his nostrils the <u>breath of life</u>; and man became a living being (Gen. 2:7 NKJ).*

The breath of life is a gift to mankind.

<u>*In Him*</u> (Jesus, the Word) <u>*was life*</u>, *and the life was the light* (energy, power of life) *of men (John 1:4 NKJ).*

The thief does not come except to steal, and to kill, and to destroy. (Jesus speaking) <u>*I have come that they may have life*</u>, *and that they may have it <u>more abundantly</u> (John 10:10 NKJ).*

Jesus speaking, *"<u>I am</u> the way, the truth, and <u>the life</u>. No one comes to the Father except through Me" (John 14:6).*

God's fifth commandment or principle is *Thou shalt not <u>murder</u>.* This is the correct translation because *kill* would exclude

24

defending life. It would be impossible. Justified homicide is different than homicide. Homicide is a deliberate and premeditated killing of a person by another person. To explain justified homicide, I would use the example of the duty of a soldier having to kill to defend his country in time of war or to kill as an act of self-defense.

God did not murder or kill anyone in the flood. It was 10 generations, from Adam to Noah, of the enemy in authority corrupting mankind until every thought and intention of man was only evil. There was no Word of God, no believing heart that would believe to hold the universe together and as a result the two firmaments, one above and one below, collapsed, and thus the destructive storms (above) and earthquakes (below).

[1]God, Who at various times and in various ways spoke in time past to the fathers by the prophets, [2]has in these last days spoken to us by His Son, Whom He has appointed heir of all things, through Whom also He made the worlds; [3]Who (Jesus) being the brightness of

His glory and the express image of His person, and <u>upholding all things by the Word of His power,</u> when He had by Himself purged our sins, sat down at the right hand of the Majesty on high (Heb. 1:1-3 NKJ).

Let me further explain. The universe is held together *<u>by the Word of His power</u>*. From the fall of man in the Garden of Eden all the way to Jesus' death, burial and resurrection, Satan had dominion, given to him by Adam. During that time, man's thoughts, attitudes, and intentions were only evil all the time.

The only words that existed came from the enemy, who had dominion and authority, and his words were lies, completely contrary to the Word of God. The enemy's words were used to prepare for destruction until man's thoughts were only evil continually.

[5]...every intent of the thoughts of his heart was only evil continually (Gen. 6:5 NKJ).

They were not thinking the Word, speaking the Word or doing the Word. Consequently, *"all things were not being upheld by the Word of His power,"* and Vov, (the 6th letter of Hebrew, also part of God's name, Yod Hei <u>Vov</u> Hei) the six-sided creation: top, bottom, left, right, front and back, of which two sides, the firmament above and the firmament below, completely collapsed. This resulted in hurricanes, volcanos, storms and destruction. These are not "acts of God". They are man's decisions, beliefs and actions that affect creation. We can take dominion over a storm, and have an effect on creation. We just don't use our dominion! (See page 73 for a complete explanation of Vov.)

Again, God had given up authority to Adam and Eve in the Garden. Satan deceived them out of that authority and ruled with killing, stealing and destroying all the way to the cross.

Jesus defeated Satan at the cross and through His resurrection left Satan resource-less. Jesus restored full authority back to mankind or *whosoever believes (John 3:16 NKJ)* to heal the sick, raise the dead and calm the storms. Jesus showed the power of authority entrusted to us. Jesus spoke to the wind and the waves to show us the authority He was investing in us.

Jesus also set the first example of using the power of God's Word to defeat the enemy when He took back authority on this earth in His 40 Days in the Wilderness. He overcame the Wilderness for us through the Word of God. If storms are an act of God, then when Jesus spoke to the wind and the waves, He was rebuking God His Father. Not so!

Question #2

Has God continually abused His bride (us) physically and emotionally from the Garden to today even after Jesus died for her (us)? Thus, does He cause sickness, disease, and grief, or does He love His bride, provide for her, heal her, and love her?

Which example should we follow?

Answer to Question #2

So, has God continually abused His bride (us) from the Garden through today? Did He abuse His people, His children, His friends and His bride as it seems to appear in the Old Testament? Did God kill, harm, hurt, starve, keep in slavery and give up on His people? Of course not!

First of all, abusiveness was done by people believing the lies of Satan to kill, steal and destroy. God did not continue abusing because He never did in the first place! He didn't abuse us. He loved us. He loved us so much He sent His only Son, Jesus, Whom He loved.

16 For God so loved the world that He gave His only begotten Son, that whoever believes in Him should not perish but have everlasting life (John 3:16 NKJ).

Sounds like a good God. Jesus presented us a loving, healing, and encouraging Father. He was building a picture of a good God. Many Christians today speak, and seem to believe, if we don't walk the straight and the narrow, God will strike us with lightening from above until we shape up or if we don't, He just kills us with a dreaded disease. Jesus is the One Who said that no one is good except God.

[18]And Jesus said unto him, "...there is none good but one, that is, God" (Mark 10:18 NKJ).

God is, was, and always will be good! That's His divine nature.

Even in the Old Testament, a not-perfect David, had a heart after God's own heart and wrote,

[6]Surely goodness and mercy shall follow me all the days of my life... (Ps. 23:6 NKJ).

David did not live a perfect life, if you've read any of the scriptures. Does this God make a way when there is no way? Does this God turn bad things into good? Think, think, think!

Question #3

Does God work hard at breaking down relationships with His own creation, His creation He gave life to? Does He do this through pain, sickness, poverty, or taking your loved ones because He needs them more than you do, and if so, for what purpose?

Answer to Question #3

I heard people, good Christians, say, "God took my son because He needed him more than me." "God took my loved one to save them from a terrible fate." What on earth would God need them for? Sweep the streets of gold? Is there a shortage of maintenance in heaven? Think!

We must stop displacing responsibility. We are accountable for our lives, and responsible for our outcome. Never give that away. God spoke it in the Garden. He gave dominion and authority to Adam and Eve. God said in the Book of Deuteronomy,

[19] ...I have set before you life and death, blessing and cursing; therefore choose life, that both you and your descendants may live (Deut. 30:19 NKJ).

Choose life! Adam and Eve chose death, and lost dominion and authority. Adam immediately displaced blame and said, "God! It was the woman you gave me." Adam invented the pronoun disease: they, them, those, him, her, he, she and it. No, it's you! Face up to it.

Again, Jesus gave us authority and dominion. We are now responsible for our life and its outcome by choices of hearing the Holy Spirit, and letting Him lead us to the light. He will never break our will. We still choose life or death.

So, maybe God's not breaking down His relationship with us. Maybe *we* are trying to hurt the relationship. But even then, we can't, because He so loved us, in the world, in our junk...

Why would He change His mind now? He made us joint heirs with His Son, Christ! He made us His children to whom He has given His very great and precious promises! We are fully qualified by the blood of Jesus for the promises 24/7.

He <u>never</u> stops loving us and sending the power of life to us.

He is the Author of love, light and life. Change your perception!

If God caused sickness and pain, then God sent Jesus to correct <u>His</u> mistake, not to correct <u>ours</u>. If God causes death, why was Jesus raised from death? Why was He healing all the sick who came to Him and raising people from the dead? Think, think, think!

Question #4

Are earthquakes, volcanoes, hurricanes, or tornadoes an act of God against man's sin? Many insurance companies call these "Acts of God".

Answer to Question #4

If God caused tornadoes, as so many believe, then Jesus was out of order in saving the lives of those in the boat by rebuking the winds and waves. In Genesis, it was 10 generations between the fall of Adam and Eve and Noah and the flood. During those 10 generations, there was no Word, no light, and no power source except Satan who had dominion and authority at that time. The key, here, is 10 generations. Yod (God's first name or Yod Hei Vov Hei) is the 10th letter of the Ancient Hebrew alphabet from which scripture comes. The meaning of Yod is extensively long. (See page 84 for the full meaning.) It is Jesus, God's

First Fruit, Jesus, the Word became flesh, Jesus, the Anointed Christ, Jesus, the tithe of God put in our hands, and Jesus, the Tree of Life, the complete assembly of God's Word.

So, when the Word is not present for 10 generations or 400 years...

**And when there is no planting
of the Word in man's heart,
all hell breaks loose!**

Look at America in 2020! We understand Hebrews 1:3,

³Who (Jesus) *being the brightness of His glory and the express image of His person, and <u>upholding all things by the word of His power,</u> when He had by Himself purged our sins, sat down at the right hand of the Majesty on high, (Heb. 1:1-3 NKJ).*

The universe is held together by His most powerful Word. And the result was two sides, of the six-sided universe, collapsed, one above and one below. These firmaments have never been redeemed.

God did not cause the flood. He was remorseful because of the lack of His Word in man's heart and life.

Also remember, God had given dominion to Adam and Eve, but Satan (Lucifer who had become Satan) stole it from them. God had to allow killing, stealing and destroying by man's choice. God had to allow man to choose by his own free will to follow after the mark of Cain (total separation from light) or the world's way, not God's way. Think, think, think!

God did not break His own commandment, *Thou shall not murder.*

How did you answer these questions?

If you answered yes to any of these questions, it's because truth has evaded you, and the lies of religion have tainted your ability to,

⁵Trust in the LORD with all your heart, and lean not on your own understanding; ⁶In all your ways acknowledge Him, and He shall direct your paths (Prov. 3:5-6 NKJ).

The Word of God and His promises struggle to work when we are in faith and fear at the same time. So <u>trusting in the Lord with all our hearts</u> will not work for us because we never know if God has good or trouble for us. You must believe God is only good and only good all the time.

Eradicate the religious lies out of your heart that affect your trust in God!

Man is and has always been accountable for his actions, but the enemy and religion has attempted to transfer personal responsibility over to God or to others. "God did it!" "My circumstances did it!" "It's their fault, my boss's fault, or the devil made me do it!" All to protect our selfish nature. The blame game is from hell and produces hell on earth. Each of us are to be accountable and responsible for our own life and eternity. Stop the pronoun disease: they, them, he, she, and it.

[1]*Therefore you are inexcusable, O man, whoever you are who judge, for in whatever*

you judge another you condemn yourself; for you who judge practice the same things (Rom. 2:1 NKJ).

A thought: those who accuse have the problem of the accusation. The accuser works full time for the devil to kill, steal and destroy. Many who accuse are doing exactly what they accuse you of.

The Word of God is for us to get rid of selfishness through accountability and responsibility for self. It is to help us to be more for others than self. We are designed to make a difference in the lives of others as well as our own lives.

A constant desire to receive for self alone creates a bottomless pit in us.

In fact, we can only receive, when we can give. Self grabs for all that life can give, but we can only appreciate what we receive when we can share it with others. Selfishness is a counterintuitive phenomenon with a gravitational pull so strong that even light cannot escape. Scientifically speaking, it's perhaps a black hole, concentrated light that can't escape. Self is never remembered by the next generation. Selflessness is always remembered in generations to come.

Selfishness will destroy your marriage, your children, your job, and your ability to live the good life God has for you because you cannot connect to the goodness of God.

So many work to advance one's own personal rights to the exclusion and loss of the rights of others.

And that is wrong and not God. Jesus was sent to redeem man from the curse of self, not the curse of God. God never cursed anyone.

If you demand your rights, it steals the rights of others and at the expense of others!

Truths to the Goodness of God
Chapter 3

In pondering the law, legalists, and religion, here is another area of review for you.

[18]For I testify to everyone who hears the words of the prophecy of <u>this book</u>: If anyone adds to these things God will add to him the plagues that are written in this book (Rev. 22:18 NKJ).

REALLY? God will add plagues?

My God adds no plagues to His kids!

John was making an Aramaic exclamation, "Don't mess with this book!"

Revelation 22:18 and 19, say *"<u>this book</u>"* and Revelation 22:19 says *"<u>the book of this prophecy</u>."* <u>Both</u> are referring to the Book of Revelation, <u>not the whole Bible</u>.

HELLO!

¹⁹and if anyone takes away from the words of <u>the book</u> <u>of this prophecy</u>, God shall take away his part from the Book of Life, from the holy city, and from the things which are written in <u>this book</u> (Rev. 22:19 NKJ).

Another Aramaic expression meaning, "Don't mess with the Book!" Think if this were really true. All translators would be headed to hell!

Could you believe that God would erase your name from the Book of Life or could John be saying, again, "Don't mess with the Book!" God has no eraser. To have one would admit He did wrong. He remembers our past no more. He forgives past, present and future sins and forgets them!

Could God erase the blood of Jesus in which your salvation is written? That would be saying that Jesus didn't pay enough.

Here is another example in the Book of Joshua.

⁸<u>This Book</u> of the <u>Law</u> shall not depart from your mouth, but you shall meditate in it

day and night that you may observe to do according to all that is written in it. For then you will make your way prosperous, and then you will have good success (Josh. 1:8 NKJ).

This Book is referring to the <u>Book of Joshua</u> not the whole Bible and is telling us of the process of taking the promises of God. The Book of Revelation tells of the end times.

A little side note on the word <u>L</u>*aw* with a capital L, as in this scripture. It is in reference to the Mosaic Regulations that Jesus fulfilled and did away with. (The Mosaic Regulations were created by man figuring that the 10 Commandments were not specific enough for every sin they could think of, so they made up 600 plus <u>L</u>aws for man to keep.) But the word <u>l</u>*aw* with a small l are the never-ending, never-changing principles of God as in the 10 Principles for a good life from a good God. Jesus speaking,

[17]*"Do not think that I came to destroy the* **<u>Law</u>** *or the Prophets. I did not come to destroy but to fulfill (Matt. 5:17 NKJ).*

Law 600-plus Mosaic Regulations
Jesus fulfilled and did away with.

*[18]For assuredly, I say to you, till heaven and earth pass away, one jot or one tittle will by no means pass from the **_law_** till all is fulfilled (Matt. 5:18 NKJ)."*

law Never-ending, never-changing
Principles of God

Pay attention, as you read your Bible, as to which meaning applies.

Continuing on, Satan, Adam, and Eve cursed themselves by themselves and did it to themselves by entering darkness, that was not created by God, but existed by man's creation. This is the part in this book where I need to explain to you the power of the universe.

God is the <u>Source</u> or Generator of all power of the universe. The worlds are held together by His most powerful Word. There is no other source of power. There is no other power energy but God's.

³Upholding all things by the Word of His power (Heb. 1:3b NKJ).

Jesus is the Word of God, the Illuminator or the Light of the world. He *is* the Light of the world. (John 8:12 NKJ)

⁴In Him was life and the life was the light of man (John 1:4 NKJ).

¹⁴And the Word became flesh and dwelt among us... (John 1:14 NKJ).

Jesus speaking:

¹²"I Am the Light of the world" (John 8:12).

Jesus, the Word, is the Illuminator of the power of God. We are the consummators or the light switch. (To consummate is the action of doing.) We now direct the power of God (as those who have dominion and authority) by faith or fear.

Faith directs the power of God to good.
Fear directs the power to darkness.

We are held accountable on this earth as to how we direct the power. Light does exist because God Is. Darkness doesn't exist until *we* give it energy, and only then, can your greatest fear come upon you.

²⁵ For the thing I greatly feared has come upon me... (Job 3:25 NKJ).

Following, are **8 Truths of the Goodness of God**. My God desires that only goodness and mercy follow you all the days of your life.

⁶ Surely goodness and mercy shall follow me all the days of my life... (Ps. 23:6 NKJ).

As stated in the Old Testament, this is God trying to say, "Hey, I'm good!"

8 Truths of the Goodness of God

Think on these statements.
Meditate on them.
Let the Holy Spirit enlighten you.

1. Only a <u>good</u> God would redeem His kids from all past, present, and future sins.

2. Only a <u>good</u> God would trust man again with dominion and authority.

3. Only a <u>good</u> God would want His kids to believe He is a good God.

4. Only a <u>good</u> God would want His goodness and mercy to follow us all the days of our lives. (Ps. 23:6)

5. Only a <u>good</u> God would make a totally good creation for man.

6. Only a <u>good</u> God would invest so much to make man and woman in His own image.

7. Only a <u>good</u> God would plan a family and Church for the delivery of His Word. That is, to teach us His character, His ultimate love and how to live an abundant life.

**Your character will determine
your fate on this earth.**

8. Only a <u>good</u> God would send His Son to redeem mankind that *whosoever believes* can become the sons of God.

[15]...<u>whosoever believeth</u> in Him should not perish, but have eternal life (John 3:13 KJV).

Notice it <u>didn't say</u> *"whosoever is good enough."*

A Few More of My Thoughts

1. I believe my God sent Jesus to redeem (*whosoever* will receive Christ Jesus) from sin: past, present, and future.

2. My God sent Jesus to take back dominion and authority from Satan, and return it to His kids.

3. My God sent Jesus to restore all that Satan had stolen.

4. My God sent Jesus to re-establish in the hearts of His kids that He is a good God, a great Father Who wants only good for His kids so we can trust Him.

**Can you now see Him and trust Him
as the God, the only God
and a good God?**

⁵Trust in the LORD with all your heart, and lean not on your own understanding; ⁶In all your ways acknowledge Him, and He shall direct your paths (Prov. 3:5-6 NKJ).

You have the power of your will to believe that God is only good and that you can fully trust Him and accept responsibility for your life and accountability for your actions.

Being blessed
is God's will for you continually.

Believe and receive health, wealth, joy, peace and favor.

In the next chapter, we'll look at a few examples that will assist you in the continuing process of knowing that our God is good.

Good God!
Chapter 4

The grace that is given to us through Christ should be proof enough that God is good and only good. As I stated earlier, the Old Testament translation has mis-translated statements. As I mentioned in Chapter 1, Kenneth Hagin researched the ancient Hebrew language and found the active verbs, many times, were translated in the causative sense when they should have been translated into the permissive sense. In other words, God did not cause but had to permit or allow. But even this implies imperfection, and God is perfectly good!

**God did not cause,
but had to permit or allow.**

Satan is the author of killing, stealing, and destroying, starting right from the Garden of Eden, where he stole authority from Adam and Eve. His stealing of authority continued on to the Garden of Gethsemane where Jesus sweat great drops of blood, and then to the cross and through the cross, death, burial, and resurrection. At that point, Jesus claimed back authority and dominion and left Satan resourceless, and then Jesus gave power, dominion and authority back to God's kids again.

The enemy stole Jesus' reputation, (turned everything, including His ministry and His disciples, against Him) killed His flesh, and destroyed His ministry, or so the devil thought. The devil tried to trick Jesus in the wilderness, but the Word (Jesus) defeated Satan there, and so it turned out at the cross. Jesus defeated him in hell, took back all authority lost and left Satan resourcesless and empty of authority with nothing but the ability to lie.

The ancient Hebrew letters contain no negatives, only the positive!

God's language is goodness only!

The Bible is God-inspired but man written. Thus we have life represented showing the results of not living by the goodness of God. And man's thoughts already had a tendency to blame God for troubles just as religion does today, thus the translation of the

Old Testament. You can truly see the difference between the Old and New Testament.

Did an unchanging God change?

Or did Jesus, the Word, only do good to eradicate man's religious opinion of God so that we can understand good and evil, and choose good by free will.

Let's look at some misunderstood examples.

⁶And it <u>repented</u> the Lord that He had made man on the earth, and it grieved Him at His heart (Gen. 6:6 KJV).

GOD REPENTED? Because God sinned?

Please! Pure light can't fall short of the power of God, His own power. Remember, there is no darkness in God. My God only sees light because darkness does not exist. When He sees no light in us, it hurts (grieves) His heart. The translators from Genesis 6:6 above, thought this (phrase, "God repented") meant that God felt sorry for God's sin.

50

Sin is to miss the power of God.
God can't miss His own power.

The translators also thought it meant God felt remorse for some wrong doing? <u>What!</u> God is good, perfect and makes no mistakes. My God can do no wrong, for He is only right. He can't sin. He is <u>pure!</u> Jesus said,

"Anyone who has seen Me, has seen the Father"(John 14:9).

And Jesus only did good.

In Greek and Hebrew, *repented* (from Gen. 6:6) means "He changed His mind." But then God is unchanging!

⁶...for I, the Lord, do not change... (Mal. 3:6).

So the best understanding is…all that took place was in the long-term plan:

- to save humanity through Noah,
- to bring a Redeemer, Jesus Christ,
- to save humanity from sin,

■to make a holy bride with a voluntary heart for Himself without spot or wrinkle!

Here is another example of a mistranslated scripture based on the ancient Hebrew.

[7]So the anger of the LORD was hot against Israel; and He sold them into the hands of the Philistines and into the hands of the people of Ammon (Judges 10:7 NKJ).

If God sold them, who paid the bill? So God got Ammon to pay him for the Israelites? Really? They're not following the principles of the goodness of God that caused all the trouble. They placed themselves in a bad position by not following God's principles.

God is always positive, happy and the ultimate joy.

God is dependent on His nature, not on man's actions!

God's plan for us is to live in His happiness and joy, and that joy is our strength (Neh. 8:10).

How about God's hatred as yet another misunderstood example? First of all, God is only love, and not capable of hate.

7...for <u>God is love</u>. (1 John 4:8 NKJ)

16For God <u>so loved</u> the <u>world</u> that He gave His only begotten Son... (John 3:16 NKJ).

It does not say, "For God so hated the world...!" So if the whole corrupt world, and its events, could not make Him mad, how does this stand? He loved us while we were yet sinners.

8But God demonstrated His own love for us, in that while we were still sinners, Christ died for us (Rom. 5:8 NKJ).

For God so loved the world that He gave His best, Jesus.

Here is a reference to hate:

5The foolish shall not stand in thy sight: thou <u>hatest</u> all workers of iniquity (Ps. 5:5 KJV).

And another,

¹³As it is written, Jacob have I loved, but Esau have I <u>hated</u> (Rom. 9:13 KJV).

Hatred is a mental sin, and God can't sin. He does not sponsor sin. He does not tempt to sin or condone sin. God is righteous and just. Jacob was just; Esau was not. Saved and unsaved may be another way of saying it, all by man's decision or will, not God's.

Jealousy, scorn, grief, and pain are human attributes ascribed to God, but cannot be God. God has none of them, nor can He have them. As Dr. Fred Price said,

**"All scripture is truly stated
not all scripture is true."**

**God has no darkness in Him.
HE IS LIGHT!**
(Emphatic)

God is righteous, perfect and just and has justified us to be a dwelling place for Himself as His bride for eternity.

Take on His mind, the mind of Christ, of only good. When you see valor or virtue in the Bible, it means "a decision in the heart to do good" and this is what God values because you seek to be like Him. Not that you always achieve it, but it's your desire and attitude that He sees. He sees the content of your heart...hopeful, filled with light, life, and love.

Ancient Hebrew Letters Reveal God's Character of Goodness and Grace
Chapter 5

The first 10 letters of the ancient Hebrew give us insight into the character of God, His divine nature. There are no negatives and no darkness in any of the ancient Hebrew letters, only God's goodness and light. They are filled with energy.

The first 10 letters speak of most of the overall creation process. The last 12 letters amplify the first 10. We will look at the last 12 letters later in this book. Each number represents a characteristic in relationship to our God, His goodness, His grace, and His character as used in the Bible.

God's wisdom has always been to communicate Who He is, Who His words are (Jesus), and His thoughts, attitudes, intentions (the Holy Spirit) for us on earth, and the process of salvation and heaven. So,

God has devised a form of letters with which to communicate that to us.

(The word *letters* in the ancient Hebrew means *signs and wonders*.) These 22 Hebrew letters assembled together in 2-5 symbols or letters give a word a meaning or a dual meaning. The meaning can exceed even more meanings, and must be discovered by the context of the word preceding and following the word. This makes a very expansive, structured language in which to understand our God, in which to live an abundant life here on earth, and in which to receive the process of salvation for eternity with Father God, His Word, the Son, Jesus, and the Holy Spirit (the feminine side of God, dare we say, *"Mother"*). Hopefully, this explanation will help you with this chapter in understanding the goodness of God revealed.

The ninth letter actually reveals ALL the goodness of God, but let's start with the first letter.

ALEPH
1st Letter of Ancient Hebrew

Aleph or one true God, one source of energy and one power stated this way:

The forward thrusting energy that seeds the universe.

There is only one source of energy in the world and/or universe: God is the I Am, and Is, and always Is. And God said,

"Let there be..."

He said it ten times in the first chapter of Genesis, and all became! The first invisible matter put together into what is seen. In the beginning God created heaven (invisible) and earth (visible).

[3]Then God said, "Let there be light" *(Gen. 1:3 NKJ).*

Light energy allows sound to travel on it. This is the root of the Quantum Theory of the

Atomic Theory or atom! Frequency makes up all matter or simply said,

"God said..." (Gen. 1).

All God created is good, created by a God of goodness. The firmament above and the firmament below were not pronounced good or bad because later man would destroy both firmaments by rejection of the 10th or the Tree of Life, explained earlier in this book.

That's a small excerpt of **Aleph**. All of **Aleph's** meanings are of a good God and only a good God.

BEIT
2nd Letter of Ancient Hebrew

Beit means duality (<u>two</u> sides) good-evil, light-dark, cold-heat. Genesis tells us that darkness was! It was not created. It was! Evil, or darkness, contains no energy, therefore it is not; does not exist until energy is given to it.

God is the Generator of Energy

**Jesus, the Word of God,
is the Illuminator, the Light of that energy.**

**You and I are the consummators,
of the Light switch.
(The activator of the Light switch)**

We direct the power as the ones who now have dominion and authority on the earth. We direct it to good or empower darkness by our decisions, acts of our will or the words of our mouths. God said we should choose life not death.

[19]...I have set before you life and death, blessing and cursing; therefore choose life... (Deut. 30:19 NKJ).

**A good God directs us to the choice of life
or the good life.**

Beit is duality but also the divine dwelling place or <u>two</u> in one. Not I, but Christ Who lives in me.

[20]...it is no longer I who live, but Christ lives in me... (Gal. 2:20 NKJ).

Through the power of salvation, saved by grace, which cleared the temple (us) of past, present, and future sins, Christ could live in a holy temple set apart for God's plans and purposes.

Male and female, that became one flesh, are duality also.

24Therefore a man shall leave his father and mother and be joined to his wife, and they shall become one flesh (Gen. 2:24 NKJ).

Sounds like a good God with a good plan.

Aleph and **Beit** are where we get our English <u>alphabet</u> (aleph-beit). English is the most closely-related alphabet to the ancient Hebrew. **Aleph** is the seed. **Beit** is the womb. God spoke the seed, His Word (Jesus), and the Holy Spirit, feminine side of God, the womb, hovered over the deep till the seed was planted, the spoken Word of God, and fruit took place, the creation!

This is an example for us today. The Word is the seed. (As God spoke the seed, we speak the seed.) Your heart is the womb. When the Word of God is received into your heart, or womb, fruit is produced! We are the Bride of Christ.

A deeper thought here is when God created heaven and earth, they were both wombs requiring seed to produce! Jesus, the Word, the Seed, must now be received by man's heart to get man to heaven. Natural seed needs to be planted in the natural earth to produce natural and supernatural fruit. So, right from the start, all is explained by a good God on how reproduction takes place for us. Jesus, the Word, the Seed, is received in our heart or womb.

Nothing is produced
without the Word.

God planted His seed, His Word. It was received, by faith, in Mary's womb, and we have the birth of Christ. The Seed of God, Jesus, Who was good, was planted in the ground (earth) after the cross, death, burial and resurrection, and on the third day produced eternal life for us. He is the first-born of the grave. This was the greatest seed planting of all.

Remember that **Aleph** is:

The <u>forward thrusting energy</u>
that seeds the universe.

Beit is:

The <u>primal receptive energy</u>,
the universal home,
the infinite womb of fertility
from which all things
are born and nourished.

GIMEL
3rd Letter of Ancient Hebrew

Gimel means trinity - three in one, the free-will giving and sharing, the goodness of God (Father, Son and Holy Spirit) always flowing the energy of the goodness of the Trinity.

Gimel emanates **Aleph** and the duality of **Beit** which makes a complete and whole person, and gives man the free will to choose good or evil, positive or negative.

Gimel also represents development, the process by which our initial spark of creativity must be properly guided so that it may flow into the physical reality, hopefully by the good we have chosen.

Gimel speaks of the existence of soul and spirit, already in the invisible, brought to life through male and female, naturally through the birth of a child. The life energy of God cannot be created nor destroyed, only changed. This is known as the Second Law of Thermodynamics. You may think you have created life, but you have only changed the energy of the female egg and the male sperm into life or the invisible into visible. Again, this is the goodness of our God, the Creator. Also the number three represents father, mother and son or daughter or $1 + 1 = 3$. (Mom + Dad + Sex = Child or 3!)

DALETH
4th Letter of Ancient Hebrew

Daleth means the **Four Realms of the Universe** and the method that God used to create it. These four realms are **Emanation, Creation, Formation,** and **Action.**

The Four Realms of the Universe

FIRST REALM
1. Emanation

Webster had a great understanding of the ancient Hebrew in defining our words in our alphabet. Webster defines the word, *emanation:*

The origin of the world by a series of hierarchal descending radiation from the God-head through intermediate stages of matter.

Wow!

This definition is found only in the early *19th Century Webster's Dictionary.* The liberal, modern translation has changed it. SAD.

Emanation, the endless, undifferentiated energy that radiates from the Creator, God, holding all things together by His most powerful Word. The Word of God is infused with His power and flows through to us. We are the light switches as consummators of the light when we believe God and walk in faith. We direct the power to the positive, to light, to healing, to wealth, to joy, to peace and to favor. However, if we doubt, fear or choose to believe a lie of the enemy, we direct the power to the negative and empower darkness or Satan who has no power unless we direct it to him. Then our greatest fear may come upon us. This is not the product of a good God. But, more the product of a bad choice of man's will and of him believing the lies of the enemy.

SECOND REALM
2. Creation – God's Dream
Encompasses the idea of creation but lacks specific forms of structure. They are thought ideas, the imaginative power of the creation, and the unseen imagining of the potential creation. This amplifies the need

for God's children to look at the unseen and not the seen.

We are to imagine a better tomorrow with faith, and expect the power to change our circumstances.

This is a vision in two-dimension waiting for formation.

[18]Where there is no vision, the people perish... (Prov. 29:18 KJV).

Yet a vision is only seen from one side without dimension.

THIRD REALM
3. Formation

Formation contains the blueprints or pattern but not the physical form. This takes on a six-sided (3-D) dimensional existence in our imagination and is the proper use of our imagination.

[8]Where there is no vision, the people perish (Prov. 29:18 KJV).

A vision is two-dimensional, a picture, the idea, yet not visible in action or movement. It's the involvement of power to the imagined picture to be meditated upon until it begins to move in the realm of a dream or formation. This realm becomes an eternal dream in color with the ability of an imaginary walk-through. Thus, this pattern comes to the verge of becoming a reality through action, the final realm, our acting on faith that God is fully employed. A good God has given us power to create a better tomorrow.

**Use God's emanating power
to envision and dream mentally
and then soon to experience reality!**

FOURTH REALM
4. Action
This is action in the dream, our faith actions. *"Rise up and walk" (Acts 3:6).* It is the invisible becoming visible reality. It's when invisible matter becomes and exists in reality or physical form. Faith

with action realizes the power of God's emanating power, illuminated by Christ and faith believed. Again, a good God's plan to be victorious in all things, a process to do good by a good God's power and our will. Remember

**A vision without action
is a hallucination,
but action without a vision
is nothing more than random activity.**

DALETH

Now, continuing on with the <u>fourth</u> <u>letter</u>, **Daleth**. Its meaning also relates to the <u>four</u> <u>rivers</u> of Genesis in chapter two, which are connected to the **Four Realms of the Universe** (Emanation, Creation, Formation, and Action) that relate to the full Gospel of Jesus.

First, each river's name relates to God's goodness and plan for mankind, all of which point out salvation and prosperity in the ancient Hebrew. When the Gospel is preached, we are to speak of <u>salvation</u>, <u>prosperity</u>, <u>success</u>, and <u>redeemed time</u>! When all of the Gospel is preached, and not just salvation, complete change occurs by those who hear what is preached. Let me say, each river represents one of the <u>four</u> meanings of the Gospel.

1. Salvation by the Blood of Jesus.
2. Prosperity, health, wealth, joy, peace, and favor.
3. Success at various levels according to our abilities - never fair and never equal.
4. Redeemed Time – not to be spent but invested.

This is the whole Gospel. (For a further study of the four rivers in Genesis, see my book, *Commentary of The Big Six of Genesis, Creation God's Way*.)

HEI
5th Letter of Ancient Hebrew

Hei is the second part of God's name and the last name of God. **Hei** Vov **Hei** Yod. (Read from left to right.)

Five is the number of grace received at salvation. **Hei** sounds like an exhale of breath.

When we breathe, we live. Twenty deep breaths will intensify colors, strengthen eyesight, improve memory, sharpen the mind, and can even bring a sense of euphoria to the flesh. Holding your breath for 30 seconds can energize the whole brain in a crisis mode which can enhance problem solving. God breathed out as He said, *"Let there be..."* and all that is in existence came from the sound vibration of His voice frequency. God breathed the breath of life into man, and he became a living soul.

> *⁷And the Lord God formed man of the dust of the ground, and <u>breathed</u> into his nostrils the <u>breath</u> <u>of</u> <u>life</u>; and man became a living soul (Gen. 2:7 KJV).*

<u>Breathed</u> means to puff CPR into, to start man breathing, or life.

<u>Breath</u> <u>of</u> <u>life</u> means that He gave:

1. <u>Intellect</u> to man.
2. The power to <u>feel</u> emotions.
3. The power of <u>the will</u> to decide.
4. The power to <u>reason.</u>

5. <u>Life</u> given by God, the Giver of Life not death.
6. Enlightenment
7. Order
8. Love
9. Concern
10. Happiness

The opposite of all of these describe those who reject God, His Word, and have received the mark of Cain. They are followers of the world and have submitted their will to the world. They have

Lost Reason
Lost Order
Lost Love
Lost Concern
Lost Happiness
Bought Abortion
Lost Concern for Others
Become Only Self-Willed
Left the right use of the human body.
Completely left God's nature and the 10 Commandments.

Sound a little like the world today?

Back to the 5th letter, Hei:

Hei is in God's name twice.
Hei Vov Hei Yod

Wow! What a good God to give so much for us! He is the Author of Life, not death. Man chose death, not God. Death, hell, and sin are all choices of man's will, not in God's plan for mankind.

VOV
God's Middle Name
HEI VOV HEI YOD
6th Letter of Ancient Hebrew

Vov – the six-sided creation: top, bottom, left side, right side, front and back to create the three-dimensional world in which we live. God created the universe in six days. Perhaps, one of the six sides was formed each day as the ancient sages suggest, front, back, right side, left side, top, and bottom.

The word *confession* begins with **Vov**. All the world was spoken aloud into being. **Vov** suggests when we accept our own uniqueness, a meaningful joining together can take place, and social networking happens. A better life can result.

A good God created a perfect universe for man's good life, but the fall of man, the lack of the Tree of Life and man destroying the two firmaments (which have not been redeemed) resulted in storms and earthquakes. The firmament above and the firmament below collapsed due to no power of the Word that holds the universe together. Neither of the firmaments were spoken of by God as good in Genesis 1. Therefore, they could collapse at the fault of man, not God. When you remove the Word of God and the 10 Commandments, watch America struggle. Why? Because America was built on the Word of God. Read your Constitution.

ZAYIN
7th Letter of the Ancient Hebrew

Zayin is the first letter in the word *time*. **Zayin** speaks of the seventh day of rest, the seven-day week, and the Church Age. On the seventh day, God rested. **Zayin**, or time, is included in creation as time! Light travels at 186,000 miles per hour. The speed of sound is 780 miles per hour. Sound travels on light to form the atomic structure (all is frequency).

Nothing exists without time. (*In the beginning...* Gen. 1:1) Time cannot be altered, changed, slowed down or sped up because it first is. Time always is. Yesterday does not exist nor does tomorrow! God always operates in the now. Jesus said now is the time of harvest. Hebrews 11:1 tells us..."*Now faith is.*" God is I Am now (Ex. 3:14). **Zayin** states,

Keep your focus on your purpose.

We lose our sense of purpose when we worry or fear. Don't fear or worry.

**Focus makes faith supreme,
and faith is the access to grace
or the goodness of our God**.

*[2]...we have <u>access by faith into this grace</u>
in which we stand, and rejoice in hope of the
glory of God (Rom. 5:2 NKJ)*.

A good God gave us the ability to forget
yesterday and change tomorrow to the better.
Thus, the power of speaking aloud the Word of
God and believing in our hearts that the
promises are ours. We are fully qualified.
Because of the grace and mercy of a good God
Whose Son took all our past, present, and
future sins to the cross, we can be a clean
temple through which Christ can live.

CHET
8th Letter of the Ancient Hebrew

<u>Chet</u> is the name or number of comple-
tion, the unending God, number of God, the
reciprocal God Who gives and receives. He
made us a receptacle to contain Him and His
Word but also made us reciprocal and able to

allow, by choice, His goodness to flow through us to others. Also all of His gifts, all of His promises are to flow to us and through us. He gives health and vitality of life to us in all of creation, and expects our life in return, by our free will, to be His eternal bride, through salvation. Praising, thankfulness, worshipping, giving, loving and imitating our God through His goodness is what should follow salvation.

Chet is the bridge between the letters **Vov** and **Zayin**. Creation, confession, saying, or speaking God's Word in the Church Age produces every good thing for us. Faith comes by hearing the Word of God, thus,

Go to church
and hear the Word.

[17] So then faith comes by hearing, and hearing by the word of God (Rom. 10:17 NKJ).

It's not about the messenger, the denomination, religious statutes, religious tradition, but it is the message being spoken when it's the living Word of God.

Chet is connected to dreams, visions, and imagination, (and seeing the invisible) and when spoken out loud, can become our supernatural structure of the dream of our tomorrow by His infused power in His Word. But we can only bring into the natural what has always existed in the invisible; the goodness prepared for us from the foundation of time by a good God.

TET
9th Letter of the Ancient Hebrew

Tet is the statement of good. All that is and was created by God is good, and that God is only good.

Good is sealed into creation.
Good is often hidden in the universe.

Wow! A letter dedicated to the fact that God is good and only good! His finished work on the cross. *"It is finished" (John 19:30)* is the greatest example of God's goodness toward mankind, completed, finished proof of His goodness.

Christ is for us in the ninth hour, a total statement of God's goodness and love for us.

[44]...*Now it was about the sixth hour,* (6th letter – creation - **Vov**) *and there was darkness over all the earth until the* <u>*ninth hour*</u> (**Tet** – goodness of God sealed) *(Luke 23:44 NKJ).*

Tet refers to the ancient text as a dazzling, divine light or energy. Goodness is the energy of God, and when His goodness is acted upon by man, from his will and heart, it brings inner clarity and emits a supernatural glow to illuminate or influence others' lives with the goodness of God. God is only good and there is no darkness in Him.

God cannot be tempted. In fact, God's goodness cannot see darkness because darkness is the absence of energy or power; therefore darkness isn't, but God is. After Adam and Eve fell, they hid in darkness and God said to Adam, *"Where are you?" (Gen. 3:9)* God asked because He can't see darkness. They went into darkness, but God could hear sound coming from darkness. He hears our prayers, but He couldn't see the sin, for God can't be tempted.

God heard the cries of His people in Egypt and sent Moses with the power to set them free, God's unmerited grace by the blood.

Let me interject a thought here as we look at the freeing of the Israelites from Egypt. In present translations, it may appear that God caused all of the plagues, when, in fact, the constant rejection of God's Word forced light back so darkness prevailed. (Pharaoh's constant rejection of the word from God, given by Moses, to set God's people free.)

15Be diligent to present yourselves approved to God, a worker who does not need to be ashamed, rightly dividing the Word of truth (I Tim. 2:15 NKJ).

To *divide* means:
a total act of doing,
to make a straight cut,
to bring to light what is God's truth and
what is man's truth.

As Dr. Fred Price stated,

**"All scripture is truly stated
not all scripture is true."**

You must successfully go with the truth, understand the truth, God's truth. So again,

**God gives life, love, and light.
The enemy kills, steals and destroys.**

The third commandment says,

⁷You shall not take the name of the LORD your God in vain... (Ex. 20:7 NKJ).

This translates, *"Don't blame God for evil."* There is no darkness in Him. God is only love, light and life. Apparently, the inspired writings of much of the Old Testament did not carry this belief into their writings. (Maybe that's why translations of the Old Testament only contain causative verbs and not permissive verbs, when in fact, it should have been translated to say God permitted or allowed and <u>not God caused</u>.)

We all only hear in part, and revelation is subject to the prophet. So we must separate God's truth, His goodness, His love and His light, from human truth, and live by God's truth.

Let's talk about the goodness of God as we look at what is perhaps the second greatest Bible translation attack on my God's goodness. (The first attack was on God's goodness as previously discussed regarding the flood. See page 23.) It is vastly believed that Moses may have penned the first five books of the Bible. These books contain so much spiritual insight into God's character, God's divine nature and God's creation process of goodness. The 10 Commandments (I call them, The 10 Principles. See page 152 for an in-depth study.) given to build a civilized society in the Promised Land, still apply today but also the human belief system of man is involved.

Let me restate for you: the enemy kills, steals, and destroys (John 10:10). The enemy had stolen authority and dominion from Adam and Eve, and so, when we read the account of Egypt and the 10 plagues, we must understand,

God <u>had</u> to allow the plagues, (the death angel, Satan) in order to free the people and plunder the wealth of the Egyptians. This wealth had been stored up by Joseph.

...the wealth of the sinner is stored up for the righteous (Prov. 13:22).

The Israelites left with the first-born of Egypt's wealth by the blood of the lamb. God's people left with none sick among them, which is the fulfillment of God's goodness and His grace and mercy or unmerited favor. They did not earn it!

Much is allegorical of our salvation today and our life in Christ. Stay in Christ, (or the Word, in His house) eat the lamb (the Word) stay protected by the blood, and in Christ, the Word, and ask for the wealth of the wicked laid up for the just. A good God shows us the way, the truth, and the life.

Tet can only cause us to understand that God is good only. All letters before number nine continue to establish the goodness and love of God for His creation and mankind.

**For He loved us even in our sin
and loves us eternally.
That's a good God!**

*⁸But God demonstrates His own love
toward us, in that while we were still sinners,
Christ died for us (Rom. 5:8 NKJ).*

YOD
10ᵗʰ Letter of the Hebrew Alphabet

<u>Yod</u> - the only letter that is suspended in
mid-air! **Yod** is a culmination of the first nine
letters of God's goodness. **Yod** is God's first
name Hei Vov Hei **Yod,** (in Hebrew, His name
reads from right to left) with this understanding, God sent His Son, Jesus, to redeem
mankind. God sent His tithe, His first-fruit.

Now grasp this! Jesus is the Tree of Life
Who was sent into the garden with Adam and
Eve. Jesus is God's tenth sent to us to redeem
us. Every time someone gets saved, God's tithe
to us is paying Him dividends. When God sent
us Jesus, His **Yod,** He sent:

NOW IN US

BRING THE WHOLE TITHE

1) Tree of Life (Jesus)
2) The Anointed Christ (Jesus)
3) God's First-Fruit (Jesus)
4) God's Word Became Flesh (Jesus)
5) Our First-Fruit, His 10th, **Yod**, Jesus brought to the House as His tithe. Not ours He gave all this to us, but all is His. **All this is now in us and of us.** We bring the whole tithe!

Now Malachi tells us to bring the <u>whole tithe</u> (not just <u>the tithe</u>).

10Bring the whole tithe into the store-house... (Mal. 3:10 NIV).

The whole tithe is what we are to bring into the house, His house, the Church, and

18...on this rock I will build My church (Matt. 16:18 NKJ).

The Rock, Jesus, in ancient Hebrew and even in Greek means:

1) Tree of Life (Jesus)
2) The Anointed Christ (Jesus)
3) God's First-Fruit (Jesus)
4) God's Word Became Flesh (Jesus)
5) Our First-Fruit, His 10th, **Yod**, Jesus brought to the House as His tithe.

He entrusted the tithe to us to bring to His house to finance His Kingdom. Then God finances yours! This is the tithe, not just money, but it is His love, forgiveness, encouragement, peace, and service which builds up, and does not tear down. All five above are to flow to us and through us continually like a river.

[1]Unless the Lord builds the house, they labor in vain who build it (Ps. 127:1 NKJ).

**Build His House.
He will build yours.**

Yod represents a supernatural messenger bringing movement and change to our lives, moving through the universe in a micro instant. It's the power/energy of movement as it acts initially and takes on greater and greater force. This is the power of faith with action, an upward movement to betterment. Science may refer to this as a photon, however it is yet unexplained scientifically. A photon best described is. God is and God is good. It's His energy. And He is everywhere even where you are now. He is! You can only find God in the now.

Yod begins the Hebrew word for *exodus* meaning marching forth, rising up or leading out. It is also the first letter of *day* in the first chapter of Genesis. This was the first full day and evening, the first day, which God said was good. The Bible never uses Saturday, Sunday, Monday, Tuesday, Wednesday, Thursday or Friday. Why? The names of all of these days of the week were named after or represent false gods.

Yod states that a single small event in a single day of our lives can exert an incalculable effect on all of creation, a word of encouragement, the widow's mite. Jesus said the two mites (two pennies) the widow gave was everything she owned, and it had an incalculable effect on creation. (See Luke 21:1-4.) By giving God the first-fruit of your day, you will change your life and others for good.

Everything that is in motion has life. Therefore, movement is a must to avoid stagnation!

The letter **Yod** represents a human force for soul change. God changed Jacob's name from Jacob to Israel in Hebrew. Israel, Joshua, Joel, John, Ezekiel, Jeremiah, and Isaiah – all these leaders' names begin with the letter **Yod**, a power to cause soul change. He also changed Abram to Abra<u>ah</u>am and Sari to Sar<u>ah</u>. In both, God added <u>ah</u>, meaning joy and laughter. <u>Ah</u> in the ancient Hebrew has its root in **Yod** or God's first name. From His name, **Yod**, He added to their names, because the sound <u>ah</u> spoken over and over has a positive effect on the changing of the soul. The unspoken name is **Yod Hei Vov Hei** meaning, Tree of Life,

Creator. We hold ourselves accountable for our actions on earth by choosing light or dark.

Yod is the first letter of impulse and also means that we are to love God with all our hearts, by impulse not analyzation. Jesus knew this letter and refers to it in Scripture:

^{37}Jesus said to him, "You shall love the Lord your God with all your heart, with all your soul, and with all your mind. ^{38}This is the first and great commandment. ^{39}And the second is like it: You shall love your neighbor <u>as yourself</u>. ^{40}On these two commandments hang all the Law and the Prophets" (Matt. 22:37-40 NKJ).

This denotes <u>selflessness</u> and <u>self</u>:

<u>Selflessness</u> - loving God with compassion and showing kindness and goodness to others.

<u>Self</u> - love yourself, marry, build a house, have children and engage in business, not for selfish motives, but for others, your

family, your church and the world.

The letter, **Yod,** is the tenth letter and relates to the ten forces comprising the universe in and around the Tree of Life. These ten forces sustain creation, renewing it through constant motion.

Let's look even deeper at the letter **Yod.** We see this letter used in the Ten Commandments and the tithe. **Yod** and the number 10 refer to the Tree of Life that was in the Garden (Gen. 2:17). Because all was created good, the goodness of God is the energy of God. Evil does not exist – it is the word for the absence of good! Just as cold does not exist, it's only a word to describe the absence of all heat. Cold is immeasurable, however you can measure the level of heat energy. *Darkness was* in Genesis 1:1. It's the word for the absence of light. Light is energy, and darkness is the absence of energy. The Tree of the Knowledge of Good and Evil was a natural tree with its roots in the natural earth drawing its life from the natural creation. God created all trees good therefore evil did not exist. (It existed only if light left.) The more God is removed from schools and government, the more darkness enters into those areas.

The Tree of Life was an inverted tree (figuratively) with its roots at the top and branches on the bottom drawing its life from God, the Creator of light and energy. Jesus, the Tree of Life, said,

[19] *"...I say to you, the Son can do nothing of Himself, but what He sees the Father do; for whatever He does, the Son also does in like manner" (John 5:19 NKJ).*

This is an ancient Hebrew image that is used to explain the Tree of Life. Man chose the natural Tree of Good and Evil instead of the Tree of Life. When you eat from the Tree of Life, you choose God's plan, His power, and His life and you are being led by the Spirit of God. If you eat of the Tree of Good and Evil, you may do good, but produce nothing or you may do bad and produce bad.

Today we should eat of the Word, Jesus, the Tree of Life. Jesus returned to redeem mankind as the Tree of Life (which has always been before the foundation of time). Remember the Tree of Life, the Word became flesh, God's First-Fruit (the 10th, the Tithe), Christ, the Anointed One, **Yod** and cannot be separated. All are one in meaning.

⁵I am the vine (tree), *you are the branches. He who abides in Me and I in him bears much fruit, for without Me* (the Word of God) *you can do nothing (John 15:5 NKJ).*

⁹And out of the ground the Lord God made every tree grow that is pleasant to the sight and good for food. The Tree of Life was also in the midst of the garden and the Tree of the Knowledge of Good and Evil (Gen. 2:9 NKJ).

And the Lord God commanded the man saying,

"Of every tree of the garden you may freely eat but of the Tree of the Knowledge of Good and Evil you shall not eat" (Gen. 2:16 NKJ).

The Tree of Life (Jesus, the Word) was there in the Garden, as was the other tree, the Tree of Good and Evil.

Man ate from the Tree of Good and Evil for self and not for building and blessing. He ate his seed or his future, the tithe of the Garden that belonged to God.

22 Then the Lord God said, "Behold, the man has become like one of Us to know good and evil. And now, lest he put out his hand and take also of the Tree of Life, and eat, and live forever..." (in sin) *(Gen. 3:22 NKJ).*

Then in Verse 24:

24 So He drove out the man; and He placed cherubim at the east of the Garden of Eden, and a flaming sword which turned every way, to guard the way of the Tree of Life (Gen. 3:24 NKJ).

God allowed man's choices to drive man out of the blessing of the Garden and a flaming sword, the Word, which man rejected, ends up guarding the Tree of Life. Man could not get to the Tree of Life. For if he ate of it, in a fallen state, he would have lived forever in the fallen state.

So, once again, man has a free choice to tithe and maintain the relationship with God. The tithe does not affect your salvation or eternity with God; it only affects the natural world blessing and the ability of the Church to build His Kingdom, His church.

The ancient Hebrew reveals that the tithe is not money, gold, or an offering of wheat, but rather, these objects are an energy of God that have the power to change man's soul or heart. Jesus said,

21 "For where your treasure is there your heart will be also (Matt. 6:21 NKJ)."

So, gold, silver, and money offerings are to be given, but understand, there is energy in them to affect your life when given to God's House, missions and the poor.

The power of giving bestowed on us by a good God.

Jesus is the Word of God, the Tree of Life, and in the born-again Christian. The Tree of Life contains 10 resistors or capacitors. A capacitor is defined as a device for accumulating and holding a charge of power. In this case, we are talking about God's power. These resistors or capacitors were set in place by a good God to guard us from His full power which we could not possibly handle at salvation. A simple example of this is when people go under the power of God during the laying on of hands. The power of God on them at that moment circumvents their physical ability to stand.

Though God put the resistors/capacitors in place to protect us, He, at the same time, wants us to grow, moving through each resistor/capacitor, to a place where we can receive His full power and energy flowing through us. Though we do have the full power in our born-again spirit, the resistors exist in the soul, which the Word is de-weeding. This is directly connected to giving and receiving.

We learn giving from a truly good God Who gave it all for us!

¹⁶For God so loved the world that He <u>gave</u> His only begotten Son... (John 3:16 NKJ)

*¹⁹We love because <u>He **first** loved us</u> (1 John 4:19 NKJ).*

He is a good God Who loved us <u>first</u>! He didn't wait for us and demand our love and affection, but He exercised His giving heart by pouring out His love on us <u>first</u> so we would respond by <u>giving</u> love <u>back</u> to Him and to others.

Life consists of giving and receiving and giving reciprocally. All forms of giving such as giving love, service, finances, and encouragement, have the ability to move us up the Tree of Life. We decide whether we will give at all, what we will give and if we will move through each level. In the parable of the sower, Jesus makes it clear God's way of growth is giving, not hiding or storing what we have.

24-25 "Listen carefully to what I am saying—and be wary of the shrewd advice that tells you how to get ahead in the world on your own. Giving, not getting, is the way (God's way). *Generosity begets generosity* (and increases life). *Stinginess impoverishes* (and steals life) *(Mark 4:24-25 MSG)."*

This is the world's way:

Get all you can.
Can all you get.
Sit on the can!

We <u>receive</u> God's love, and we become responsible to <u>give</u> God's love. We <u>receive</u> encouragement from the Word, and we are responsible to <u>give</u> encouragement to others. We <u>receive</u> financially, and we are responsible to bring our first-fruits into the House of God, and <u>give</u> financially. The more we grow in giving, the more resistors we are working through, and the closer we grow to the power of God moving in and through us. As our capacity increases to give, we increase our capacity to receive power. So our good God is drawing us closer and closer to Him by our giving.

He is never trying to take from you.
This is His way of <u>getting more to you</u>!

Getting money to you not from you! When you give, it's given to you! That's a good God!

³⁸Give, and it will be given to you; good measure, pressed down, shaken together, and running over will be put into your bosom. For with the same <u>measure</u> that <u>you use</u>, it will be measured back to you (Luke 6:38 NKJ).

You could say *the measure that <u>you use</u>* is the resistor/capacitor you are working through to get to the next level of giving.

Below are the 10 Levels (resistors/ capacitors) of Giving in the ancient texts that must be accomplished to live in all the full power of the blessings of God. We live in 1%

reality and 99% invisible reality. To live through the 99% invisible reality, all 10 Levels of Giving are required, and this is ultimately where God wants us to be. So these 10 levels of the Tree of Life are growths which explain the process of the promises and how the greater power of God is released as we give. This interpretation is taken from Bible scholars of old who took from the meaning of this Hebrew letter, **Yod**.

All giving is acceptable to God. Each level fulfilled carries you higher and higher up the Tree of Life with continued increase in power available.

This is the goodness of God!
He shares His power with us
to live life more and more abundantly.
GOD IS GOOD!

10 Levels of Giving
(10 Resistors/Capacitors to Grow Through)

1. **Begrudging Giver**
   "I don't want to, but I will."

2. **Under Giver**
   "I give less than I should and less than I can afford, but I'm happy to make some contribution."

3. **Reactive Giving**
   "I can help those close to me happily, (but not the House of God)."

4. **Proactive Giving**
   "I see need, and I give (to people or church, the House of God)."

5. **Uncomfortable Giving**
   A stretch outside comfort – giving more than you feel comfortable giving. This is sacrificial giving, and it is good for the soul.

6. **Giving without Recognition- Anonymous Giving. (Care for others.)**
This non-ego giving is ranked high in God's sight.

7. **Giving Without Demanding a Return. (Care for others.)**
You give for the sake of giving. You feel good for doing it, so it's also ranked high in God's sight. (God loves a cheerful giver 2 Cor. 9:7.)

8. **Proactive Giving (Care for others.)**
You anticipate the need of the Kingdom and give before the need arises, to (and or through) the local church.

9. **Global Scale Giving (Care for others.)**
You give beyond the local church through the local church to reach beyond the walls of the church to the world globally – mission consciousness.

10. All 9 Levels of Giving Together is the 10th level of Giving

Always ask yourself where you stand on the scale of 1-9. Clarity and truth are the devil's greatest enemy. When you act in truth, you don't have to wait to give with the right motive. Remember God can only protect what you own, not what you owe.

**So <u>all</u> forms of giving in grace
are accepted and blessed
because of the blood of Jesus.**

Now we are understanding the Tree of Life and what this Tree is (yes, it's the Word and yes, it's Jesus), but let's go deeper than that. (See the Tree-of-Life diagram on the following page.)

Tree of Life

"Study Me," Jesus said.

THE TREE OF LIFE
JESUS, THE WORD
JESUS THE WAY, THE TRUTH, AND THE LIFE

The Hebrew says of the
tree of good and evil in the garden,
you are your own source.

GOD-GRACE
Energy-Power
Emanation
Yod Hei Vov Hei

John 15:7
Abide in the tree,
Jesus, and I abide in
you, the Word.

*Power flows
to creation*

**Tree of
good and evil**

Holy
Spirit
Mother
Female

Father
Jehovah
Male

Balance

Wisdom
Led by Spirit
Live by Faith

Natural Power

Draws substance
from natural flesh

Mind
Intelligence
Creation

Son
The Word
Jesus

Understanding
Power of Thoughts,
Words & Actions
lined up with the
Word of God

Baptism of
Holy Spirit

Draws substance from God,
the source of power, not you.

Power of the Word

Emotion
Formation
Feeling

Knowledge
Positive or
Negative-Choices
Virtue-Choice of doing good

Seeking
Wisdom
of God

Tithes & Offerings
cause upward growth
from salvation

Giving in all forms
moves you up the
tree of life to greater
power and blessings.

Baptism of
Holy Spirit

**Tree of life is
an inverted tree**

Body
Action
Salvation
Prayer of repentance
and receiving Jesus
in your heart

Salvation of soul
& spirit, born again

YOU

*Redeemed growth
closer to the
source*

Narrow Way: Matt 7:13
Enter through the narrow gate. For wide
is the gate and broad is the road that leads to
destruction, and many enter through it.

You are here at salvation.
You grow up from here,
by the power from God to you.

Material World 1% — Invisible 99%
Kingdom of God and the Promises take the invisible and
makes things visible through the Tree of Life, the Word.

103

The Tree of Life, explained by the ancient sages, showed an inverted tree. The explanation is that the Tree of Life (Jesus, the Word) drew its power from heaven, Father God, the invisible flowing through the vine to the branches to produce fruit.

The Tree of the Knowledge of Good and Evil was a normal tree deriving its natural power from the natural earth. If we were to explain the Tree of Life today, it is no longer a tree in the Garden of Eden, but is now living in the born-again Christian. Therefore, its roots draw its power from the born-again spirit. Jesus *is* the Tree of Life!

⁵I am the vine, you are the branches... (John 15:5 NKJ).

This is the Word working through our soul to quicken our mortal body to produce fruit into the natural world from the spirit by faith in the Word of God.

The scholars of old illustrated the Tree of Life to help man understand it. The sages of ancient times taught this.

The Tree of Life is inverted from the natural trees on earth. Its roots are on the top, feeding its way down from God's energy, and God's power. We are returning energy by praise and worship, thankfulness, prayer, right living, the tithe, offerings and missions, by the power of the Word, back to God. This completes the reciprocal action of returning light to its source (God) so that it is again made available to us to receive the power to prosper. It is a continuous flow, if not interrupted by fear or selfishness, both of which make self the source, instead of God.

The spiritual climb of this tree is an upward climb to the roots or God, the Creator. As we increase our spiritual competency, by ascending up each level, we increase our spiritual capacity to absorb more and more light through the process of giving, not just financially, but giving love, encouragement, service, etc.

Once we've received Jesus (the Christ, the Light of the world, the Life), the Tree of Life, Jesus is in us.

The Tree of Life is *in* the born-again Christian.

But the Tree of Life has transforming levels or the capacity to protect us from the infinite light and power of God. The power or the energy is transformed down to a manageable level of light and power that we can handle. As we grow up toward the Source (the roots) of the Tree of Life, we gain capacitors (the capacity) to retain more energy/light.

As we look at the chart, we see three columns (right, left and center) reaching down from the Godhead to the natural world. The right column is positive/masculine, the left column is alternative/feminine (though it does not mean less than) and the center is a balance of the two. (Think of a cross: right is masculine, left side of the cross is feminine and the center is Jesus. Grace is at the top and salvation is at the bottom.) Through the mediation of both the left and right columns, making them both equal in good and empowered to do good, and thus the connection to the Word, Jesus became flesh to make salvation available.

Digging New Roots
Chapter 6

The Tree of Life is divided into four worlds as discussed in the fourth Hebrew letter, **Daleth**. I spoke of this in-depth in Chapter 5, but here is a short summary of each of the four worlds:

1. **Emanation**
2. **Creation**
3. **Formation**
4. **Action**

1. **Emanation** – the radiating power and energy flowing from God to make, retain and hold together creation - ...*upholding all things by the Word of His power... (Hebrews 1:3 NKJ).* God is the Generator of all and only energy in the universe.

2. **Creation** – the world of intelligence, intellect, ideas, imaging, two-dimensional vision. *Without a vision My people perish (Prov. 29:18).*

3. **Formation** – the emotional world, detailed with feeling, three-dimensional, as a dream; an imaginary walk through an imaginary world of desires of tomorrow.

4. **Action** – the material world, the actions of believers activating the power of God in an instant or to move invisible to visible, with faith, and God seeing the content of light energy in your heart.

10 Stations of the Tree of Life

The Tree of Life has ten stations representing spiritual growth. (See Tree of Life Diagram on page 103.) We begin with Station 10.

Station #10 of the Tree of Life

God, Creator of all undifferentiated potential - a blazing light and intelligence Who sends all energy and light to the whole Tree of Life, the Word, Jesus, the Light of this world.

Station #9 of the Tree of Life
Wisdom beyond reasoning - the universal <u>good</u> Father God, beyond human comprehension.

Station # 8 of the Tree of Life
Understanding universal good Mother which contains all energies of life that motivates and nourishes human endeavor and keeps the galaxies spinning. This is the feminine side of God, the Holy Spirit. He created man and woman in His likeness, image and spirit. This, and the prior two stations combined, unifies energy through understanding and transmits it to knowledge. Knowledge is the beginning. Seek knowledge. However, you need to move up and seek understanding also. Seeking knowledge only, produces intellect, and intellect, without understanding, produces one who can't believe God.

Most importantly, seek wisdom. It is the ladder up the Tree of Life. Adam and Eve sought knowledge and not the next level up of understanding so they could then get to wisdom and not eat of the Tree of the Knowledge of Good and Evil.

Had Adam and Eve sought understanding, they would not have eaten the natural tree and would have tasted of the Tree of Life.

Jesus is the Author of life and goodness.

Station # 7 of the Tree of Life

The energy of mercy and unrestricted desire to share - generous to a fault. This is associated with the Sabbath, the seventh day of rest, or the Church Age, which we are in now. Jesus died for His Church. Because of His sacrifice, we enter His rest when we believe the Word, do the Word and give into the local Church. The Church can then show mercy and an unrestricted desire to share with the lost and needy. This is why 100% of God's people should be tithing so that God's plan can be carried out, the goodness of our God with a good plan.

Station #6 of the Tree of Life

This carries the energy of judgment and restriction. It demands a consequence to our actions, the implementation of cause and effect. It is the counter balance to overflowing generosity. Never give all to get all. Be sure before you ever give all, that you heard clearly from God, or you could end up poor.

Never give in to debt.
Get out of debt.

Giving of all is ok if you don't give into credit or by the flesh. Only give all if you are sure that you heard from God and not from the flesh. This is the first significant block to our being overwhelmed by the light of the Creator. Unrestrained energy of any kind can be destructive on our part. Think about the light of a nuclear blast. Moses could not see all of God; only a part of Him, and he glowed for days! God's goodness.

Station # 5 of the Tree of Life

The energy of beauty and ideal balance - symmetry - the heart of the Tree of Life - the balance of discernment and mercy (love, light, life). <u>God's goodness</u>.

Station # 4 of the Tree of Life
The energy of victory and life - a desire to share life and bring that desire to the physical realm - the link between God and man - male and female, the sharing of life to create life (the sperm and the egg to create a life). This is a part of the right-brain process. It is romance. It is the dreamer, the artist, the masculine fertilizing principle. Mating and procreation desires to be controlled within the marriage commitment. The womb has the power of selection. <u>God's</u> <u>goodness</u>. Women have the power of selection of seed. They have always had the power of choice, but after they have chosen seed, they lost the power of choice and now have committed to the harvest or the birth.

Station # 3 of the Tree of Life
The feminine side - the egg in human conception controls a voluntary process, and the left brain activates the steering - the practicality of the conception, the potential of the male's desire is controlled by the female's acceptance

to procreate. It is the female's decision to receive or reject. As I mentioned, the power of selection is <u>God's goodness</u>, where a woman has a choice. Once she chooses seed, she is responsible and accountable to and for that seed.

Station # 2 of the Tree of Life

The foundation, a great reservoir that mixes the above attributes and pours them into the world of action (yet the light is never unbearable to us in the physical world). Relationship of <u>God's goodness</u>.

Station # 1 of the Tree of Life

The starting place of salvation; the action of believing Christ as Savior. The lowest part of the Tree is referred to as the Kingdom of God when we enter at salvation. And He lives within us, those who are in the material world, in Spirit. It's a house (our bodies, a temple) that houses God, the Son and the Holy Spirit within. Obviously the <u>supreme goodness of God</u>.

Our bodies are empowered to build His house provided we lovingly desire to build it. When our body is placed in the House of God (a church), God's House grows and the gates of hell will not prevail against it. (Matt. 16:18 NKJ). Yet again, as with the first Adam, the Tree of the Knowledge of Good and Evil resides along with the Tree of Life allowing us a decision of living in the light or in the darkness by choosing which Tree we choose from which to eat. Through the letter **Yod**, we see the importance of the number ten.

There are ten levels of spiritual growth intertwined with the ten levels of giving, the Ten Commandments (when lived by, produce life) and the giving of one-tenth, the tithe (an energy that empowers life more abundant, the changing of the soul). When the tithe is given into God's storehouse, where His name resides, (the local church you attend) that seed becomes incorruptible. Now the 90% that you have left cannot be stolen because it's protected by the energy of your giving. All that is left, is now incorruptible. Giving is the way to grow up the

Tree of Life, and your increase must exceed ten percent.

**Tithing protects what you own, and
the offering is the sign of a loving heart
inclined to build God's Kingdom
as the Spirit leads and deserves a
30-60- or 100-fold return.**

For more revelation on the benefits of tithing, see my books, *Releasing the Blessings You Can't Contain* and, *Where the Blessings Are/TENS.*

He is Unchangeable
Chapter 7

As I mentioned in the beginning of this book, we will now look at the 12 remaining letters of the ancient Hebrew that continue to give us clues to God's character, love and concern for us. Again, making the statement,

God is only good, always was good, and always will be good.

All of the ancient Hebrew letters lead us to the Tree of Life, Jesus, the Messiah.

KAF
11th Letter of Ancient Hebrew

Kaf is the first letter in crown. Crown refers to the crown of the Tree of life, God's love, mercy and grace. This is the supreme or highest of the energies making up the Tree of Life.

Power	Grace	Love
Holy Spirit	Word	Father God
Mother	Jesus	Jehovah
	Only Believe	

This energy is beyond human comprehension. **Kaf** gives us direction in Christ, the Tree of Life, to intentionality, human will power, one-pointedness, single-mindedness, or focus to pray with intention and purpose.

13And He said to them, "It is written, 'My house shall be called a house of prayer,' but you have made it a den of thieves" (Matt. 21:13 NKJ).

Many distractions can affect your personal temple of prayer (your heart) as well as keep you from going to church. Distractions of want of other things can affect your giving, your serving, your concern for the Kingdom and God's people.

**Stay focused on good,
all His goodness.**

Do not set aside your growth up the Tree of Life with greater and greater powers. Faith comes by hearing and hearing the Word of God, and how will they hear, unless the Word is preached in His House.

LAMED
12th Letter of Ancient Hebrew

Lamed teaches us not only to know the truth but also to understand the truth so we can be doers of the truth. We don't do what we know to do, but we do what we understand to do! This is called wisdom, doers of the Word of the Tree of Life.

Lamed is an understanding heart.

As Solomon asked, not for things, but for a heart of wisdom to judge right or left (ha ha) or good or evil.

An understanding heart is:

1. Cunning and crafty use of resources, (beneficial investments) word, time, money, love, goodness, etc.

2. Discerning - ability to know good and God's will without the use of natural senses, not see, hear, taste, smell, touch.

3.   Perceiving - to yield to a higher authority, the Word, the Holy Spirit. It is the ability to submit, not who to, but able to.

4.   Concerning - care about others a little more than yourself. Life is to be about others, not self. When you demand your rights, it will be at the expense of someone else's rights.

5.   Giving – having and seeing needs, and a desire to meet them, and investing your life in building the Kingdom of God and your life as well. A good God gives us wisdom freely.

**In giving,
we imitate the goodness of God.**

Lamed also advises us to watch what we vocalize. Be not like a fly who seeks sores. Don't judge, hold offense or cling to unforgiveness. None of these are good and stop good from coming to you. They are a wall to the soul.

MEM
13th Letter of Ancient Hebrew

Mem represents the lost sea of human consciousness including intuitive knowledge, sensitivity and the depths of thought concealed from view that are seldom considered or acknowledged. It's a stream of thought that flows forever. The deeper we go into this area of thought, the greater the flow of wisdom and ability to be led by the Holy Spirit. The use of meditation amplifies the depth of thought.

Mem is the first letter in angel and messenger. Your offering given sets up a spiritual connection and allows the messenger to bring spiritual insight and revelation that is life changing. Revelation is when, in thought, a knowing is released to us spiritually. It's when you know that you know or fully understand.

Full understanding is real revelation.

Mem relates to the number 40 – 40 days in the wilderness, 40 years in the wilderness, 40, the length of time to fruitfulness. Do good for 40 days and experience a good thing in your life.

Only 40 days to a new good habit, a new life.

A good God gives a good path of life.

NUN
14th Letter of Ancient Hebrew

<u>**Nun**</u> – this relates to the number 50. Joshua represents Yeshua, Jesus. Joshua was the son of Nun. **Nun** represents the 50th day of Pentecost in the upper room and the Holy Spirit's entrance. Fifty is the Year of Jubilee which is the Church Age of every day, every year, now. (Be happy; don't worry.) It is the return of all things lost.

Nun, an Aramaic word for fruitfulness (the sign of a fish) and faith that brings abundance to our lives. **Nun** relates to melody or tune, the right sound or vibration. Music is a spiritual force. Music with words is finite limited and ends with textual conclusion. In-tune music without words is endless and raises us into transcendent heights and spirituality.

Music opens the gate of the invisible to strengthen your faith and elevate you to spiritual inspiration. The walls of Jericho fell by sound. The universe was built with sound and frequency. A good God reveals truth.

**Enjoy good music,
the kind that lifts you up.**

³Then God said, "Let there be..." (Gen. 1:3 NKJ) Sound frequency then entered the energy of light.

SEMECH
15ᵗʰ Letter of Ancient Hebrew

Semech is the first of the ten stations of the Tree of Life. It's the bottom of salvation where we start at being born-again. (See Tree of Life Diagram Page 103.)

Semech has secrets in hidden realms around us! Revelation from the Word of God by illumination. God reveals these things as we grow in the Word of God.

Semech is a hedge of protection around us in our homes, and that protection is doubled when we are planted in the local House of God, His house. God hand-planted a garden with a hedge of protection around it, in Eden, a picture of the Church, with another hedge of protection around the church, *and the gates of hell will not prevail against it (Matt. 16:18).* This is double portion.

Semech encourages story-telling. It's a way of waking people up from a subconscious slumber. Jesus used parables to change our soulish realm. When emotion is added to an experience, it will never be forgotten.

**A good God assists us
in remembering good.**

AYIN
16th Letter of Ancient Hebrew

Ayin is the interaction of perception, insight, and the gift of discernment. The ability to know something without the five natural senses (hear, see, taste, touch, and smell). Growth up the Tree of Life is created by growth out of self with more and more concern for others or simply put, giving of self to others. Demanding selfish rights will steal the rights of others.

Ayin tells us that by the power of meditation on the words of God, by God's power, we attain perceptions of profound mysteries which cannot be completely expressed in human words. It's understanding by the Spirit.

A good God empowers us for good.

Ayin states through salvation we are in the Tree of Life and it is in us, and we are now a Tree of Life.

With Christ in us, we no longer live
but the Tree of Life,
the All in all is in us!
I in Him and He in Me.
(John 17:23)

PEI
17th Letter of Ancient Hebrew

Pei, more often than any other letter, represents the power of Adam's speech which

God gave him for authority and dominion. Adam and Eve lost that authority and dominion to the enemy but it was restored to mankind by Christ, and now our speech is empowered to speak life or death.

**As a good God,
God recommends speaking life.**

Human speech sets and releases spiritual energy into the universe. It's an energy which sets both visible and invisible events into motion. So we should see that silence has virtue at times. An example is, as an ancient sage states, *"To shame a person in public is akin to murder."* Be careful, accusers. Remember accusers have the problem of the accusation. The log is in their own eye.

**There is power in the spoken Word of God.
Use it or lose it!**

TZADI
18th Letter of Ancient Hebrew

Tzadi represents God righteousness lent to man by the cross, death, burial, and resurrection of Christ Jesus. It is meant to produce, through salvation, a person who embraces family, friends, community and responsibility in God's House. This is one who brings light, the love and goodness of God down to this rocky, mundane world. This is a person who has gone up the transforming levels of the Tree of Life and conveys to others the true perception of God and all His power.

Tzadi is a person who can bend his will to submit to God's will for his life.

Tzadi is one who gives, serves cheerfully, compassionately and comforts with understanding and doing so anonymously is the highest form of goodness. The goodness of a good God flowing through you! Light up!

KUF
19th Letter of Ancient Hebrew

Kuf is a compound of **Zayin** (focus on purpose) and **Reish**, a higher consciousness, through the Holy Spirit, of great intuition and/or discernment! This is a gift of the Spirit, the breathing in of the breath of life by the Holy Spirit in God's House. Only a good God would empower us, His kids, to receive these gifts and fruit of the Holy Spirit: love, joy, peace, patience, goodness, kindness, gentleness, faithfulness and self-control. The goodness of God for a good life.

REISH
20th Letter of Ancient Hebrew

Reish is associated with a higher conscious, stating that we are all capable of great intuition. Fear and anger are the only obstacles to achieving this greater consciousness. The fullness of the Holy Spirit can take you to higher levels of spiritual consciousness, giving strong influence into what to do for tomorrow, foresee dangers and have discernment and allowing soul changes by the Word of God. A pure set up for us from a good God.

SHIN
21st Letter of Ancient Hebrew

Shin speaks of shalom: health, wealth, joy, peace, wholeness and prosperity, all the makeup of a good God. **Shin** is His divine nature, a God of goodness. *Be ye partakers of the divine nature of God (2 Pet. 1:3-4 KJV).*

Shin speaks of entering His rest and the empowerment of what you say. Find harmony through meditation on the Word of God. Continual soul change by the Word of God.

Shin is the Sabbath, the Church Age. Now every day is the Church Age or the Sabbath. Jesus is the Sabbath. We are to enter His rest because all is paid for by the Blood of Christ.

[27]And He said unto them, "the Sabbath was made for man, and not man for the Sabbath: [28] Therefore the Son of man is Lord also of the Sabbath" (Mark 2:27-28 NKJ).

In this age, we are to make all personal attempts by the power of our will to be happy daily and to do good.

**This leads to wholeness
and concern for others,
the goodness of God.**

TAV
22nd Letter of Ancient Hebrew

Tav is the final letter of the Ancient Hebrew alphabet. **Tav** speaks of our universe being in existence and operating in cycles of all things from life to death. The end of human life on earth is joyful. The complete redemption in Christ Jesus is the great fulfillment of the Sabbath, the eternal rest of God.

In creation, the nature of God fell into all of creation (all which is good) by a good God, all held together by His Word, (Col. 1:17, Heb. 1:3) His divine nature.

**Tav speaks of fervent prayer,
to pray the Word with great passion.**

Ask = demand.
Seek = dig as for treasure.
Knock = knock the door down. Take the
　　　　Kingdom by force (Matt. 11:12).

Tav speaks of forgiveness, a place to walk in continually, which never hinders the blessings of a good God. God has a continual flow of forgiveness to us, but unforgiveness, judgment and offense can stop the flow. You stop the flow. Your belief in darkness blocks the light. It's not a good God stopping the flow.

Tav speaks of doing excellent in all our endeavors to cause constant flow of light energy to us.

Do good.
Receive good.

The Good Abrahamic Covenant
Chapter 8

The Abrahamic Covenant is the Covenant of Grace that Jesus, Who was full of grace and truth, settled for us through His death and resurrection, by His blood.

...the glory of the one and only Son, Who came from the Father, full of grace and truth (John 1:14 NIV).

This Abrahamic Covenant, the Covenant of Grace was <u>between</u> <u>God</u> <u>and</u> <u>Jesus</u>, His Word. It was not like the Old Covenant that was <u>between</u> <u>God and man</u>. The Old Covenant was the law, not grace, and man was unable to keep this covenant. The making of the Abrahamic Covenant was God working with Abraham. God caused Abraham to nod off to sleep so Abraham could not mess it up.

**All that would be required of Abraham,
and ultimately us,
would be to believe God and not doubt.**

Abraham saw and believed and received a form of salvation in grace, and it was credited to him as righteousness.

²¹ and being fully convinced that what He had promised He was also able to perform. ²² And therefore "it was accounted to him for righteousness" (Rom. 4:21-22 NKJ).

⁷Therefore know that only those who are of faith are sons of Abraham. ⁸And the Scripture, foreseeing that God would justify the Gentiles by faith, <u>preached the gospel to Abraham beforehand</u>, saying, "In you all the nations shall be blessed." ⁹So then those who are of faith are blessed with believing Abraham (Gal. 3:7-9 NKJ).

In essence, this says God <u>preached the Gospel of Jesus to Abraham</u> beforehand and, Abraham believed and received the grace of the covenant.

It was no longer about his behavior in life but about believing what God said.

The disciples asked,

²⁸… "What shall <u>we do</u>, that <u>we may work</u> the works of God?" (John 6:28 NKJ)

²⁹ Jesus answered and said to them, "This is the work of God, <u>that you believe in Him Whom He sent</u>" (John 6:29 NKJ).

That you believe in Him Whom He sent. He sent His Word, His tithe, His First-Fruit, His Son, Jesus (the Seed of Life) and His 10th to this earth to lend His grace and mercy to mankind, because man was incapable of living right in the flesh but was capable of believing.

Believing causes obedience.
Obedience does not cause believing.
Think about it.

God is either trying to find you or has found you and wants to lend grace and mercy to you. The process of growth in the Tree of Life, the Word (Jesus), to the blessed life in His grace, is found in Genesis 12:1-4:

¹Now the LORD *had said to Abram:*

"Get out of your country, from your family and from your father's house, to a land that I will show you. ² I will make you a great nation; I will bless you and make your name great; and you shall be a blessing. ³ I will bless those who bless you, and I will curse him who curses you; and in you all the families of the earth shall be blessed" (Gen. 12:1-4 NKJ).

Again, that blessed life in His grace is not obedience but believing.

²⁶... faith without works is dead also (James 2:26 NKJ).

¹Now the Lord had said to Abram: "<u>Get out</u> of your country, from your family and from your father's house, to a land that I will show you" (Gen. 12:1 NKJ).

<u>*Get out*</u> in the ancient Hebrew relates to salvation. God preached the Gospel to Abraham.

135

[8]And the Scripture, foreseeing that God would justify the Gentiles by faith, <u>preached the gospel to Abraham</u> beforehand, saying, "In you all the nations shall be blessed." [9]So then those who are of faith are blessed with believing Abraham (Gal. 3:8-9 NKJ).

Abraham had to believe to receive to *get out*. He had to *get out* of worldly thinking and the world's way. (Jesus is the Way, the Truth, and the Life, John 14:6.) Abraham was in the midst of the cradle of civilization, the old Eden, which had been abandoned, Iran and Iraq of modern day. That is an area of confusion, death, poverty, false gods, and corruption, still today.

God has always wanted to bless His creation and give us the best life possible on earth. In order to do that, we submit to His way, not ours. We take our thoughts captive and *think on these things* (the goodness of God).

[5]...we <u>take captive every thought</u> to make it obedient to Christ (2 Cor. 10:5b NIV).

[8] ...whatsoever things are true, whatsoever things are honest, whatsoever things are just, whatsoever things are pure, whatsoever things are lovely, whatsoever things are of good report; if there be any virtue, and if there be any praise, <u>think on these things</u> (Phil. 4:8 KJV).

Abraham was asked to *get out* or leave his beliefs in false gods, wrong family perceptions, and worldly ways.

Next, God said to Abraham,

[1] "Get out of <u>your country</u>..." (Gen. 12:1).

This relates to our wilderness of "just enough" also "just-enough thinking". Most people work hard to just make it past the 30 days of the month and the bills. "Thank God! We made it!" But God's plan for us is to live life and life more abundant (John 10:10). He has only increase on His mind for us. Jesus became poor that we might be rich.

[9] For you know the grace of our Lord Jesus Christ, that though He was rich, yet for your

sakes He became poor, that you through His poverty might become rich (2 Cor. 8:9 NKJ).

The only people God says, "Well done, my good and faithful servant" to are the investors of money, the multipliers of money. Luke 19 is a money chapter. Watch closely.

¹²...A certain nobleman (Jesus) *went into a far country to receive for himself a kingdom and to return. ¹³So he called ten of his servants, delivered to them ten minas,* (Each mina is equal to 3 months' salary) *and said to them,* (Jesus said to them,)
"Do business till I come."
¹⁴But his citizens hated him, and sent a delegation after him, saying,
"We will not have this man (Jesus) *to reign over us." ¹⁵And so it was that when he* (Jesus) *returned, having received the kingdom, he then commanded these servants, to whom he had given the money, to be called to him, that he might know how much every man had gained by trading.*

Only three out of ten of his servants showed up. The rest ate their seed.

¹⁶ Then came the first, saying,

"Master, your mina has earned ten minas."(10 times) ¹⁷And he said to him,

"Well done, good servant; because you were faithful in a very little, have authority over ten cities."

¹⁸ And the second came, saying,

"Master, your mina has earned five times."

Five times, or in translation, as I said before, "Well done, good and faithful servant."

¹⁹Likewise he said to him, "You also be over five cities."

²⁰Then another came, saying,

"Master, here is your mina, which I have kept put away in a handkerchief. ²¹For I feared you, because you are an austere man. You collect what you did not deposit and reap what you did not sow."

²²And he said to him,

"Out of your own mouth (you will be judged) *I will judge you, you wicked servant. You knew that I was an austere man, collecting what I did not deposit and reaping what I did not sow.* ²³*Why then did you not put my money in the bank, that at my coming I might have collected it with interest?"*

²⁴*And he said to those who stood by,*

"Take the mina from him, and give it to him who has ten minas."

²⁵*But they said to him,*

"Master, he has ten minas."

The church is saying, "You can't take from the poor and give to the rich."

²⁶*For I say to you, that to everyone who has will be given; and from him who does not have, even what he has will be taken away from him (Luke 19:12-26 NKJ).*

This is not the way the modern church thinks, but this is how God thinks.

Again, this is the world's plan to make you a worker bee and pay you just enough to help make them rich. I call it "working for the man."

We were meant to be kings in God's Kingdom not slaves to the world's system or the world's kingdom.

Though we may work there, it's an attitude of expectance and faith. God's plan is found in the first chapter of Genesis.

28Then God blessed them, and God said to them,

"Be fruitful and multiply; fill the earth and subdue it; have dominion over the fish of the sea, over the birds of the air, and over every living thing that moves on the earth."

29And God said,

"See, I have given you every herb that yields seed which is on the face of all the earth, and every tree whose fruit yields seed; to you it shall be for food (Gen. 1:28-29 NKJ).

So God's plan is to be fruitful, (build a business, work for seed) multiply, invest in the earth and the House, the Church, and He will protect what you own and multiply your money through what you planted in the earth.

Bring your tithes and offerings into My storehouse, (the Church) and I will bring you opportunities for wealth and protect your stuff and multiply the grain and fruit you planted in the earth. That's a paraphrase of Malachi 3:10-12.

10"Bring all the tithes into the storehouse, that there may be food in My house, and try Me now in this," says the LORD of hosts,

"If I will not open for you the windows of heaven and pour out for you such blessing that there will not be room enough to receive it. 11And I will rebuke the devourer for your sakes, so that he will not destroy the fruit of your ground, nor shall the vine fail to bear fruit for you in the field," Says the LORD of hosts;

12"And all nations will call you blessed, for you will be a delightful land," says the LORD of hosts (Mal. 3:10-12 NKJ).

Leave your worldly attitude of
just enough.

Back to Abraham and the second part of God's command to him.

[12]Now the LORD had said unto Abram,
"Get thee out of thy country, and from thy kindred, and from thy father's house, unto a land that I will shew thee" (Gen. 12:1 KJV).

In the King James, it says Abraham is to leave his *kindred*. In the ancient Hebrew, this relates to your pedigree, your culture, or your heritage. Leave Italian, African, Indian, your false beliefs, your background, your habits, your pride of heritage and become a Christ(ian), a true child of God. Leave the DNA of your kindred, the bad heart, cancer, diabetes, etc.

Hook up to the DNA of Father God
as joint heirs with Christ Jesus
in health, wealth, joy, peace, and favor.

Jesus had to leave His earthly family heritage. He only did and said what His Father God did and said (John 12:49-50).

^{12}...*get out of...your <u>father's house</u>... (Gen. 12:1 NKJ).*

And God's last command to Abraham was to *get out of your father's house.* This speaks of family bondages. Most families develop behavioral patterns of the world's psychology such as lost child, scapegoat, black sheep, and/or hero, all of which divide and are a form of judgment, profiling which form bondages. Also out of these, come victims, rescuers, and persecutors, all of which produce dysfunctional adults. (For more information, read my mini book, *Name of the Game of Life, Victim, Enabler, Persecutor, Helper*)

This would also include what I call the Five Fatal Sins that hinder the life in the promises:

1. Greed
2. Lust
3. Rage
4. Pride
5. Self-ambition

These are things the Word of God desires to change in our lives to live in the Kingdom and in leaving the world system behind. The world system only brings death and destruction, but the Word hooks us up with God's system, Jesus, the Word, and the way of love, joy, peace, patience, goodness, kindness gentleness and self-control. These produce wealth, health, joy, peace, and favor through God's love and promise to take us to a promised land of great abundance, too much. So, we are blessed to be a blessing! This will cause you and your family to be great (a great nation), and your name to be great, a great reputation for generations to come.

²I will make you a great nation; I will bless you and make your name great; and you shall be a blessing (Gen. 12:2 NKJ).

This is God's plan for each of His kids, who are called by His name, to live, experience and have. It's His promise of a great life, a great name, and a great inheritance. We are joint heirs with Jesus on earth and on through eternity, both planned from the foundation of time.

**He created heaven first from the invisible
and from it, created earth, the visible,
knowing the end from the beginning,
all to prove He is good!**

Why Does Sin Oppose God?
Chapter 9

God does not look at man's sin or shortcomings the way man does. Look at the response God had for Cain (who murdered his brother) or His response toward David's adultery. We are not looking for justification for sin, we are looking at God's response versus man's response.

Why is God anti-sin?
Think about it.

It's because sin is what
keeps you from His promises.

It's not because God is being mean and wants to beat you up. That's why the scripture says,

⁸There is therefore now no condemnation to those who are in Christ Jesus... (Rom. 8:1 NKJ).

So if you feel condemnation, you have exposed yourself to the law and not to the grace and goodness of God. This does not justify sin, because the grace of God teaches us to say, "No" to sin.

[11]For the grace of God has appeared that offers salvation to all people. [12]It teaches us to say "No" to ungodliness and worldly passions, and to live self-controlled, upright and godly lives in this present age (Titus 11-12 NIV).

Has anyone asked the question, "What is sin?"

[23]...for all have sinned and fall short of the glory (power) *of God (Rom. 3:23 NKJ).*

Glory and power are interchangeable words. Most translations use the word *glory* when in fact the word *power* would be more appropriate. God has empowered the Holy Spirit to lead you to good or the goodness of God.

So what is sin? The Greek explains sin as,

**Shooting at a target and
missing the bull's eye.**

The Hebrew explains it as,

The choice of darkness over light.

Sin is when we believe the enemy, which is faith in fear, and empowers in the killing, stealing and destroying. Sin cannot be categorized as one being worse than another.

**The truth is,
sin is sin,
and
not one sin is worse than another.**

When you miss the bull's eye, you've sinned. This, of course, is why Jesus had to pay for our past sins so Father, Son, and Holy Spirit could live in a clean temple. He also paid for our present sins so He could remain in us. He had to pay for our future sins so He could stay in us tomorrow and not forsake us, otherwise you would be living in constant fear of loss which would be total condemnation.

So let's go back to what is *falling short of God's glory* or light or energy or goodness or life or love...and there you have it! If it doesn't bring love, life or light, it is falling short of His power or glory. That's sin!

Drinking, smoking, movies, mixed swimming, dancing, overeating, skydiving, watching television, Hollywood, Las Vegas, long hair on men, pants on women . . . and the list goes on and on, <u>none</u> of which applies to sin or falling short of the power of God.

Yet, anything that could shorten your life or affect someone else's life negatively is falling short of the power of God.

Excessive behaviors or addictions that harm you and/or another fit into the category of sin. Accusers, slanderers, outbursts of rage, gluttons, gossipers, and revilers fall short of the power of God because He gave us the most powerful force on earth to overcome. He gave us the power of the will, self-control, and He gave us His character which gives us His grace and His mercy to improve our behavior and learn to love unconditionally.

God identifies His classification of sin in The 10 Commandments or what I call, The 10 Principles of God. And it really is obvious to me that these 10 Commandments are the foundation upon which all the civilized world is built. I say the 10 Principles because...

If they were commandments, you would <u>have</u> to obey them to get to heaven!

But you don't have to obey them. You can live like hell if you like. You can steal or you can kill, but it's not going to go well for you here on earth. However, when followed, the 10 Principles will bring you a better life.

The only real commandment, but, again, it's not a commandment, the only real, solid, principle that applies to all 10 is to love like Jesus loves, which is the fulfilment of the 10 Commandments, (but now what I call the 10 Principles).

[34]A new commandment I give you, <u>that you love one another</u>, <u>as I have loved you</u>, that you also love one another (John 13:34 NKJ).

You are to love *as Jesus has loved*, and if you love like Jesus, you will follow the 10 Principles (Commandments). You will not do any of them against anyone, against God, or against yourself.

10 Principles for the Best Life

1) *³Thou shalt have no other gods before Me (Ex. 20:3 KJV).*

    Don't love anyone or anything above God or before God! "Let Me be in you."

2) *⁴Thou shalt not make unto thee any graven image, or any likeness of anything that is in heaven above, or that is in the earth beneath, or that is in the water under the earth (Ex. 20:4 NKJ).*

    Don't submit the power of your will to anything or anyone but God. This covers addictions and religiousness that controls your will. They become generational to the third and fourth generations. The New King James' translation uses the words, *graven images*. In other words, don't worship anything dead.

3) ⁷*Thou shalt not take the name of the Lord thy God in vain (Ex. 20:7 KJV).*

Don't blame God for any killing, stealing or destroying. This is a misuse of His name. The word *vain* has to do with vanity, lifting yourself above God and blaming God for evil. There is no darkness in God, and no darkness can be of God.

4) ⁸*Remember the Sabbath day, to keep it holy (Ex. 20:8 KJV).*

The Sabbath is now every day. Jesus said,

⁸*For the Son of Man is Lord even of the Sabbath (Matt. 12:8 NKJ).*

Jesus is the Sabbath. The Sabbath is the Church Age or the seventh day where the Word works for those who believe it and enter His rest (Heb. 4). The Sabbath is blessed 24/7, 365 days a year.

Here's a thought: Do you ever see the days of the week mentioned in the Bible? The Bible does not mention our calendar days of the week such as Sunday, Monday, Tuesday, etc. It only mentions a day called the Sabbath, the first day of the week. It also uses the words, *days* and *nights*, but it never mentions our calendar days. Natural man has named the days of the week, the first day being Sunday after the sun god. Monday was named after the moon god, etc.

5)   *[12]Honor thy father and thy mother: <u>that thy days may be long upon the land</u> which the Lord thy God giveth thee (Ex 20:12 KJV).*

Honor (care for) your parents, deserved or undeserved. This is for <u>you</u> so it will go well with you and long life is promised.

³That it may be well with you and you may live long on the earth (Eph. 6:3 NKJ).

They gave you life, the greatest of gifts!

6)   *¹³Thou shalt not kill (Ex. 20:13 NKJ).*

Thou shalt not kill is a poor translation and has led to a passive Christian population. It should read, *Thou shalt not murder, or take life without just cause.* It's the difference between justified homicide and homicide. Justified homicide is in defense of life. Homicide is because... a thousand reasons.

7)   *¹⁴Thou shalt not commit adultery (Ex. 20:14 NKJ).*

Adultery has a very extensive meaning. Adultery can be physical, spiritual or emotional. Jesus said,

⁴A wicked and adulterous generation seeks after a sign... (Matt. 16:4 NKJ).

He used the word *adulterous*. This same word, *adulterous*, in both Hebrew and Greek means: *you have chosen another god and you are having an affair with another entity other than God.*

Don't enter into spiritual, emotional or physical relationships outside your marriage. I am not coming against relationships because there are many different levels of relationship, but there is a level of relationship with the opposite sex that a husband and wife must avoid. Sharing deeply emotional things with a person other than your spouse will lead to a stronger soul tie to that person than the one you should have with your spouse. Never count on someone else's emotional support more than your spouse. You should not elevate someone else on a spiritual, emotional or physical level above your spouse. This will keep you away from dysfunctional relationships. Trust is a must. The spiritual, emotional and physical in relationships are designed to make a marriage one flesh (which really means one complete person).

8) *15Thou shalt not steal (Ex. 20:15 KJV).*

Don't take, manipulate, con or seduce anyone out of what is theirs to become yours, including time, labor, emotions, finances, and taxes.

9) *16Thou shalt not bear false witness against thy neighbor (Ex. 20:16 KJV).*

Don't accuse anyone of anything without two or three other witnesses of the truth. Generally accusers have the problem of the accusation with no support.

2Therefore you are inexcusable, O man, whoever you are who judge, for in whatever you judge another you condemn yourself; for you who judge practice the same things (Rom. 2:1 NKJ).

Accusers have changed their relationship with God to a relationship with Satan, the father of accusations. Unfounded accusations sent Jesus to the cross. The Ancient Hebrew sages makes the statement, *"Accusations are akin to murder."* The murder of character, reputation and the murder of life. People have a tendency to believe what they hear first without hearing the truth.

10) *17Thou shalt not covet thy neighbor's house, thou shalt not covet they neighbor's wife, nor his manservant, nor his maidservant, nor his ox, nor his ass, nor anything that is thy neighbor's (Ex. 20:17 KJV).*

Don't envy. It's connected to selfish ambition, and where there is selfish ambition, you will find <u>every</u> evil work. (James 3:16)

Selfish ambition is best described as every effort in life to benefit self which works 100% against the wisdom of God. Solomon (who became the most powerful, wealthiest king in the world and led his nation by God's goodness and wisdom) asked for an understanding heart. God gave him an understanding heart. This is what an understanding heart is:

The Five Principles of God to an Understanding Heart

1) Cunning and crafty use of resources (beneficial investments) which pay dividends such as love, encouragement, and finances.

2) Discerning good and evil.

3) Perceiving which (in Hebrew) is the ability to submit to a higher authority.

4) Concerning - concern for others more than yourself.

5) Giving is counter-intuitive to self and the fleshly nature. It's critical to success in life. It's God's plan of seed time and harvest. No seed, no harvest.

[16]For where envy and self-seeking exist, confusion and every evil thing are there (James 3:16 NKJ).

Every evil work is everything that counters God. Evil is a terrible force of wishing you had what someone else has instead of rejoicing over what someone else has. We should always rejoice over someone being blessed.

That's The 10 Commandments or the 10 Principles for the Best Life! All the civilized world is built by these 10. Again, I reiterate, break them, and you have no civilized society. As we have withdrawn these from our schools, our courts, and our homes, we have what's going on in America today. Uncivilized nations don't live by any of these. Civilization deteriorates as we leave the principles.

God made these principles, and gave them to the rebellious Israelites when they said they could live by God's laws.

[8]All that the Lord has spoken, we will do (Ex. 129:8 NKJ).

So <u>they</u> wrote over 600-plus articles of law to make themselves live up to the 10 Principles/Commandments, but they could not keep them.

**God had to send a
Redeemer to cover for us.**

Not a Conclusion
Chapter 10

I call this "Not a Conclusion" because the truth is only continuing to expand our understanding that God is only a good God.

I have full understanding for myself
that God is only good,
always was, is and will be good.

He created only good. He has only good on His mind for each of His kids. He sent Jesus in the flesh, His Son, or as Jesus said,

"If you've seen Me, you've seen the Father God" (John 14:9).

Jesus only did what He saw His father do. He only said what His Father said, which was only good. Of course, because Jesus is what God said, the Word became flesh. Jesus, the Father and the Holy Spirit are only good. The Holy Spirit only leads us to what Jesus said. Jesus is God's example of His profound goodness by His accomplishment for us through the cross and resurrection.

This is God's empowering goodness.

Jesus went about healing the sick, raising the dead, feeding the hungry, loving the hurting, setting captives free, improving the quality of life for everyone with whom He came into contact (Acts 10:38). Thus, this is the divine nature of God. This is His unchanging character. This is our great I Am, our Source of Life, our Redeemer, our Everything we need. This is good and gives us the keys to the Kingdom. Receive God's goodness, and experience a good life provided by the blood of Jesus.

It's a complete price paid
for us
to have the good life
God provided.

Sow His goodness and reap His goodness
by living the good life.

In conclusion,

**I believe and receive my God is only good
with good thoughts,
good intentions
and eternal love for me.**

Do You?

YOUR
PAST,
PRESENT,
AND FUTURE
ARE
CLEAN SLATES

...if you have asked for forgiveness and
received Jesus as Lord and Savior.
(See Prayer on Page 172 if you haven't!)

A Short Excerpt from
My God is Only Good
Book 2

There is something I feel I need to clear up to assist in understanding the perception that God is good and there is no destruction in Him. This will also aid in our perception of the Bible.

In 700 B.C., the Assyrians captured the area surrounding Nazareth and brought the influence of the Aramaic language. The Aramaic language is a very expressive language and sounds harsh but means soft. It sounds large but only expresses excess.

Understanding this very expressive Aramaic language will also help change our perception of the Bible without changing the Bible.

There are dozens of examples in the Bible, but I will only give a few. I encourage you to study this for yourself.

Aramaic Expression
Example #1

When God told Abraham, he would be the *father of many nations...*

⁵No longer shall your name be called Abram, but your name shall be Abraham, for I have made you the father of many nations (Gen. 17:5 NKJ).

Included with this promise was that his descendants would be as numerous as the stars in the sky and the sand on the seashore...

¹⁷...I will...make your descendants as numerous as the stars in the sky and as the sand on the seashore (Gen. 22:17 NKJ).

This meant: because this is Aramaic, simply "many descendants." You could not put that many descendants, *as the stars in the sky and as the sand on the seashore,* on the earth!

Aramaic Expression
Example #2

Jesus speaking,

[39]"...whoever slaps you on your right cheek, turn the other to him also" (Matt. 5:39).

The misunderstanding of this scripture has harmed a lot of good men.

It simply means: "Don't argue religion. You can't change someone's beliefs in an argument."

Aramaic Expression
Example #3

When Jesus said,

[30]"And if your right hand causes you to sin, cut it off and cast it from you; for it is more profitable for you that one of your members perish, than for your whole body to be cast into hell" (Matt. 2:30 NKJ).

This means: "Don't steal what belongs to another."

Aramaic Expression
Example #4

[29] *"If your right eye causes you to sin, pluck it out and cast it from you; for it is more profitable for you that one of your members perish, than for your whole body to be cast into hell" (Matt. 5:29 NKJ).*

This only means: "Don't envy what another has."

Aramaic Expression
Example #5

[18] *...they will pick up snakes with their hands; and when they drink deadly poison, it will not hurt them at all... (Mark 16:18 NIV).*

You can handle snakes, and drink any poison?

This meant: "Don't let accusations get in you. Don't be offended, and keep the enemy under your feet."

I don't know why we don't translate these things appropriately. It sure has caused a lot of controversy in the Church and in the hearts of many who have turned away from God and the Church because of these harsh and incorrect translations. The Aramaic is extreme. Jesus spoke in Hebrew and Aramaic. He would use the Aramaic extreme statements to make a serious point.

The radical Imams and Ayatollahs of the Islamic religions are using the literal translation of the Koran to radicalize the radical. "Cut the heads off the westerners," the Koran states in Aramaic, but means, "Don't associate with the West because it will get on you." But these radicals are being trained up in the literal translation of killing and want to destroy the West.

There are some things we must get right
so we can understand, trust and love,
in return,
a good God Who loves us,
died for us and
wants us to be blessed
to be a blessing.

Did you enjoy, *My God is Only Good*?

If this book touched your heart, and you want to read more, I recommend you read my wife, Dr. Maureen Anderson's, book, *God's Grace Fuels My Passion*. Learning about God's grace reveals a good God! A life-changing book!

Go to www.maureenanderson.shop.

PRAYER OF SALVATION

Salvation does not mean following a bunch of rules to try to keep God happy. The truth is that He loves you and wants you to experience joy, health, peace and prosperity. You can only do that knowing Jesus as a Friend and Savior.

How can you be saved? It is a matter of simply believing. The Bible says: *If you confess with your mouth the Lord Jesus and believe in your heart that God has raised Him from the dead, you will be saved.* (Romans 10:9)

If you believe, then pray this prayer:
"Dear Father God, I ask you to forgive me of all my sins. Jesus, come into my heart, come into my life, be my Lord and Savior, in Jesus name, amen. Jesus is Lord!"

Congratulations! You made the very best decision you have ever made or ever will make. Now you are saved. You are forgiven and you are on your way to heaven. The next step is to grow in this new relationship with God. The best way to do that is to read your Bible every day so that God can speak to you through it and then get involved in a good church so that you can have support and fellowship of other believers.

We would love to hear from you!
If you received Christ as your personal Savior, we want to send you a free Bible. Email us at Thewordforwinners@gmail.com or visit us on line at becomingamillionairegodsway.com

Enjoy watching the Andersons teach?
Visit **maureenanderson.TV** and
becomingamillionairegodsway.TV

MORE BOOKS BY THE ANDERSONS

Dr. C. Thomas Anderson
Visit **becomingamillionairegodsway.shop**

Becoming a Millionaire God's Way Part 1
Becoming a Millionaire God's Way Part 2
Becoming a Millionaire God's Way Workbook
Will the Real America Please Stand Up?
No More Sacred Cows, Grace > Religion
LOL Your Way to Life – Anecdotes and One-Liners to Get
    You through Your Day
Releasing the Blessings You Can't Contain
Intelligence by Design
Personal Growth to Power – Jesus between the Lines-18
    Power Principles to Success
The Big Six of Genesis
Mind Over What Matters
The Money System, Are You Being Dumbed Down?
Essence of Creation – 7 Principles
Please Train Up Your Child/Character Determines Your
Child's Destiny
Where the Blessings Are

Dr. Maureen Anderson - Visit **maureenanderson.shop**
God's Grace Fuels My Passion
God's Grace Fuels My Passion Workbook
God's Grace Fuels My Passion CD Set
Releasing the Miraculous Through Fasting with Prayer
Are You Spirit Led or Emotionally Driven
Damaged DNA
Making Impossibilities Possible
Confession of God's Word (Leather)
Releasing Miracles by Speaking God's Word

How to Hear from the Holy Spirit (Mini Book)

Both Drs. C. Thomas and Maureen Anderson
Marriage Beyond the Dream
Health God's Way
Name of the Game, Victim, Enabler, Persecutor, Helper

Join The Word for Winners Family today!

Yes, I want to join Drs. Tom & Maureen Anderson in the Word for Winners partnership. Enclosed is my first offering of $ _____ to establish my monthly partnership and help reach the world with the Word of Grace.

_____ Please contact me to show me how to receive my free e-book for becoming a monthly partner.

Name _____

Address _____

City

_____

State _____ Zip _____

Phone (_____) _____

Email _____

_____ I would like to set up an automatic gift from my debit or credit card.

_____ I would like to donate one time today.

Card Number _____ Code _____

Expiration Date _____

Name on the Card _____

Send to: The Word for Winners
               P.O. Box 22229
               Mesa, AZ 85277

I sow this seed in faith believing that God will meet my need:_____

_____

Thank You!
If you would like prayer, call the prayer line, 480-669-0102.
www.thewordforwinners.com

175